LICENSED 1

A Field Manual for Mortifying Sin

Brian G. Hedges
Cruciform Press | Released July, 2011

To my sons, Stephen and Matthew:
May you triumph over sin through the gospel of our
crucified and risen Savior.
– Brian G. Hedges

Print ISBN:	978-1-936760-23-7
ePub ISBN:	978-1-936760-24-4
Mobipocket ISBN:	978-1-936760-25-1

CruciformPress.com
email: info@CruciformPress.com
Facebook: http://on.fb.me/Cruciform
Twitter: @CruciformPress
Newsletter: http://bit.ly/CruciformNL

"Are there things you hate that you end up doing anyway? Have you tried to stop sinning in certain areas of your life, only to face defeat over and over again? If you're ready to get serious about sin patterns in your life – ready to put sin to death instead of trying to manage it – this book outlines the only strategy that works. This is a book I will return to and regularly recommend to others."

Bob Lepine
Co-Host, *FamilyLife Today*

"Sanctification is a grueling process. But it's NOT the process of moving beyond the reality of our justification but rather moving deeper into the reality of our justification. This is why when Jesus was asked in John 6:28, "What must we do to be doing the works of God?" he answered, "This is the work of God, that you believe in him who he sent." Jesus was getting at the root of the problem because justification alone kills all of our self-salvation projects that fuel all of our bad behavior and moral failures. Brian Hedges shows the importance of fighting the sin that so easily entangles us and robs us of our freedom by fleeing to the finished work of Christ every day. Well done!"

Tullian Tchividjian
Pastor of Coral Ridge Presbyterian Church and author of *Surprised by Grace: God's Relentless Pursuit of Rebels*

"Brian Hedges hasn't written a book for our recreational pleasure, but a 'field manual' to assist us in our battle against sin. Rather than aiming at simple moral reformation, *Licensed to Kill* aims at our spiritual transformation in this fight by addressing the "drives and desires of our hearts." Like any good field manual, this is a small volume that focuses on the most critical information regarding our enemy, and gives practical instruction concerning the stalking and killing of sin. This is a theologically solid and helpfully illustrated book that not only warns of sin's danger, but also holds out the gospel confidence of sin's ultimate demise."

Joe Thorn
Author, *Note to Self: The Discipline of Preaching to Yourself*, Lead Pastor, Redeemer Fellowship, Saint Charles, IL

"Are you ready for a serious fight to the death? My friend Brian Hedges goes for the jugular by dusting off a near antique word (and worse, a scarcely-used yet lethal weapon): mortification. Are Christ-followers really licensed to kill? Read this "field-manual" and you will discover that you have a monstrous and aggressive antagonist who is aiming to annihilate you. It's your duty to fight back! Brian has given us a faithful, smart, Word-centered guide to help us identify and form a battle plan for mortally wounding the enemy of indwelling sin."

Wes Ward
Senior Director of Media & Content Strategy, *Revive Our Hearts* (and a co-elder with the author)

Table of Contents

One

KILLING SIN

The Definition of Mortification

Cory Byrne was showing off his pet. Draped over his neck and shoulders was his nine-foot-long, twenty-five-pound boa constrictor. To the horror of a watching friend, the reptile's large, lumbering coils began to tighten around its owner like a noose. Slowly, irresistibly, the great snake squeezed Cory's life away. His air supply was cut off. His face turned red and he passed out. Unable to remove the snake by herself, Cory's friend called for emergency help. But several hours later Cory died in a local hospital.

Some animals cannot be tamed. You may call a snake your pet and give it a cute name, but that doesn't take the wild out of it. No matter how long you've housed, cared for, and fed a boa constrictor, it may still turn on you. After all, it is still a snake.

It is much the same with sin. You may cuddle sin like a pet, but that doesn't take the wild out of it or make it less dangerous. Evil cannot be domesticated. Sin is poised to attack your faith at any moment. Sometimes it bares its fangs and strikes in a surprise attack. Sometimes it is cunning enough to play dead and subtle enough to pose as something good. But either way, sin is wired to kill. Slowly, cleverly, when you're not paying attention, sin will squeeze the faith, love, and holiness right out of you.

This is the nature of sin. Left unchecked, it always destroys. Sin's hostility is both unchanging and fatal. Sin defiles the human conscience, hijacks human relationships, and weighs down the world with brutality and injustice. Worst of all, sin creates a gulf between us and God. Our intention towards sin must therefore mirror its hostile intentions towards us: death and destruction. This was precisely Paul's point when he wrote, "if you live according to the flesh you will die, but if by the Spirit you put to death the deeds of the body, you will live" (Romans 8:13). Or in the words of seventeenth-century pastor John Owen, "Be killing sin or it will be killing you."[1]

Theologians of past generations, following Romans 8:13 in the KJV ("if ye through the Spirit do *mortify* the deeds of the body"), called the duty of killing sin *mortification.* We do not often use the word *mortification* today. When we do, we usually mean humiliation. If I say, "Michelle was mortified," I mean that she was really embarrassed about something. But Paul isn't talking about being embarrassed. When he commands us to "mortify the deeds of the body" he has one thing in mind: killing sin. That's what this book is about.

Licensed to Kill is intended to serve you as a field manual for mortifying sin. But this isn't the kind of field-manual a backpacker or naturalist might carry. There is nothing so tame as bird-watching or collecting butterflies in the pages that follow. This is more like the field-manual of a covert intelligence agent. The context is war and the goal is survival. K̲i̲l̲l̲ ̲o̲r̲ ̲b̲e̲ killed. What we need is detailed instruction on surviving a dangerous assignment while in aggressive and hostile enemy territory. With that aim in mind, each chapter of this book will:

- address an important aspect of this gritty but necessary business of killing sin;
- explore a key passage from Scripture about mortification;
- and conclude with a series of "Examine and Apply" questions .

In this first chapter we will define and clarify what mortification actually *is* by setting it in contrast with what it is *not*.

Mortification Is About Indwelling Sin, Not the Physical Body

Some people associate mortification with the medieval Roman Catholic practice of "mortification of the flesh," which employed ascetic techniques such as self-flagellation and wearing rough clothing. Others equate mortification with less severe forms of asceticism, pre-scribing vows of fasting, solitude, poverty, or celibacy as the path for fighting sin—as if food, companionship, possessions, or sex were evils in themselves.

But Scripture cautions against this approach to spirituality. Paul alerts us to the danger of false teachers who "forbid marriage and require abstinence from foods that God created to be received with thanksgiving" (1 Timothy 4:3). In another passage, he warns against those who say, "'Do not handle, Do not taste, Do not touch'" with the goal of promoting "self-made religion and asceticism and severity to the body" (Colossians 2:21–23). These people advocate spiritual advancement through a lifestyle of bodily renunciation. But Christianity is not against the body. As C. S. Lewis said,

> Christianity is almost the only one of the great religions which thoroughly approves of the body—which believes that matter is good, that God himself once took on a human body, that some kind of body is going to be given to us even in Heaven and is going to be an essential part of our happiness, our beauty, and our energy. [2]

No, our physical bodies are not evil. God made the body and sent his Son to redeem it.

What, then, does Paul mean when he says, "If you live according to the flesh you will die, but if by the Spirit you put to death the deeds of the body, you will live" (Romans 8:13)? By "the flesh," Paul doesn't mean the physical body, but indwelling sin, the sinful disposition of the fallen human nature. By "deeds of the body," he doesn't mean *all* the deeds of the body, but those that are sinful.

This is the obvious interpretation when we compare Romans 8:13 with two other verses. Colossians 3:5 says, "Put to death therefore what is earthly in you: sexual immorality, impurity, passion, evil desire, and covetousness, which is idolatry." This list of sins clarifies that when Paul says we should put to death "what is earthly in you," he means sinful deeds and desires. This interpretation is even clearer in Galatians 5:24, which describes our relationship to sin in terms of crucifixion. We'll take a closer look at why Paul compares mortification to crucifixion in chapter 7, but for now notice *what* he says is crucified: "And those who belong to Christ Jesus have crucified the *flesh* with its *passions* and *desires.*"

So, "the flesh" is our fallen and sinful disposition towards evil, which has passions that war against the desires of the Spirit (Galatians 5:17), and those desires must be killed. The focus of mortification, then, is not our physical body, but our sinful desires and the sinful deeds they produce.

Mortification Targets the Heart, Not Just Behavior

If we want to kill sin, we must aim at the right target. That target is not merely bad behavior but the sinful desires of the heart that produce the behavior. Mortifying sin will certainly bring about changes in what we say and do, but we need more than external reformation. Many people change their behavior without changing their heart to any significant degree. But Jesus is concerned about the root and motivation of sinful behavior—our drives and desires—not simply the behavior itself.

For example, Jesus denounced the most religious people of his day, the Pharisees, for their externalism and hypocrisy. He said that they were "like whitewashed tombs, which outwardly appear beautiful, but within are full of dead people's bones and all uncleanness. So you also outwardly appear righteous to others, but within you are full of hypocrisy and lawlessness" (Matthew 23:27-28). You can't always tell what's going on in the heart by looking at behavior. Sometimes we present a fine moral exterior that actually conceals inward evil and corruption.

This emphasis on the heart means that we must be careful in our assumptions about sin, whether our own sins or the sins of others. We should not assume that the lack of certain behaviors means that sin is mortified or the heart is pure. Just because someone is no longer given to certain kinds of sins is no indication that his heart has been changed. John, for example is enslaved to food. On the surface, this is a sin of the appetites, the sin of gluttony. John may become self-disciplined through diet and exercise, and lose a lot of weight, but that doesn't *necessarily* mean that the deeper root of sin has been mortified in his heart. For John may still be bound to the sin of selfishness. Once his sin took the form of overeating. Now it may take the form of vanity and an over-concern about appearance. The expression of sin was pruned away in one area, but because the root was left intact, a different expression simply grew up in another location.

Here is another example. Jennifer never indulges in angry outbursts or vindictive behavior. She appears to be as calm as a still lake on a cool, cloudless day. If you met her, you would think: "Wow. She is really peaceful—like Jesus." But those who know her well understand that this peaceful exterior is due to her placid personality, not any particular working of grace in her heart. While Jennifer appears calm and never struggles with anger, the truth is that she frequently falls prey to fear, anxiety, and cowardice. She never gets mad at anyone, but neither does she confront others when she needs to. Her life is a web of codependent relationships, and she is the enabler. [3]

You see, sin expresses itself in different people in different ways. That's why measuring external behavior in one area alone simply isn't enough to determine the state of one's heart. The only way to kill sin is to mortify the roots of sin in the motives, desires, and drives of the heart. But to detect these desires we have to look comprehensively at our lives. You can't measure holiness by simply taking one or two slices of behavioral patterns. In the two examples above, if you only focused on behavior in one area of John or Jennifer's life, you could easily be misled. You could think, "here is a tree that produces only good fruit." But that would be a false assessment, based on a surface judgment. We simply have to dig deeper. And one of the aims of this book is to help us with that task.

So, mortifying sin is not merely changing behavior, but rather addressing sinful desires in the heart. But *how* are sinful desires weakened?

Think for a moment about the act of killing. How do you kill something? To make this more palatable, let's consider snakes again! There are lots of ways to kill a snake. You can crush it with a rock, starve it, burn it, drown it, or chop off its hideous little head. Choose your favorite method, but what you're essentially doing in each is depriving the snake of something it needs to live—be it brains, food, air, or a hospitable environment. That's what we have to do with sin in the heart. We have to *weaken* sin by taking away the things that give it strength, by depriving it of food and air, as it were. This means that one of the most practical ways to kill sin is to quit giving it opportunities to thrive: "Make no provision for the flesh, to gratify its desires" (Romans 13:14b). We'll return to this topic in the next chapter.

Mortification Leads to Progressive Holiness, Not Sinlessness

What is the goal of mortification? What does "kill sin" actually mean? It's an important question, because our expectations ought to be aligned with what God *intends* and what Scripture *promises*. If we aim too low, we will dishonor God and regularly miss out on important opportunities for growth in holiness. If we demand more of the process of mortification than the Bible says we can expect, we set ourselves up for discouragement and defeat.

The goal of mortification is a life of genuine holiness that results from the gradual weakening of sin's influence in our hearts and lives. Notice that this is clearly different from the total removal of sin from our hearts. Do not be mistaken: mortification does not produce perfection in this life.

Of course, we *desire* sinless perfection, and we should. And the Lord has purchased this for us. Someday we will be like him, conformed to his image in every way

(Romans 8:29, 1 John 3:2). But while perfection is our ultimate desire, we will not attain it this side of glory. We will contend against indwelling sin all our days in this life (Romans 7:14–25). This means that life on earth is marked by warfare: "Beloved, I urge you as sojourners and exiles to abstain from the passions of the flesh, which wage war against your soul" (1 Peter 2:11). We are engaged in a lifelong battle.

This reality shouldn't discourage us, but it should make us vigilant. Imagine you are a foot soldier at war in enemy territory. Your squadron faces daily skirmishes against enemy soldiers who are experts in guerrilla warfare. Though the fight is brutal and fierce, you know you are on the winning side. Victory is on the horizon. This confidence keeps you from losing hope. But the daily danger keeps you from dropping your guard. So you study the strategies of your enemy. You watch the perimeter of your base. You maintain the best defenses possible. You keep yourself always armed for battle.

This is how we must engage in the war against sin. We need to study the strategies of our enemy. We need to know ourselves and our weaknesses. And we must always be armed with our spiritual weapons.

So when you see an exhortation to "kill sin," resist any impulse to think you can deal a once-and-for-all death blow to your sinful nature. *Mortification* is an umbrella term for a whole range of activities designed to gradually weaken the power of sin in your life — the range of activities we will spend the rest of this book examining.

Mortification Is for Believers, Not Unbelievers

You might expect Jesus to require more of unbelievers than he does believers. But here, as in so many other areas, the Lord turns our expectations upside down. He *invites* non-Christians to come to him, and offers them *rest* for their souls (Matthew 11:28–30). But to us, we who claim to love and follow him, Jesus demands drastic measures in dealing with our sin. Paul's teaching reflects the same emphasis. The scriptural commands to put sin to death are always addressed to those who already believe in Jesus.

This tells us two things. First, as we saw above, Christians still have to deal with sin. The Bible holds out no illusions of moral perfection in this life. But second, this underscores the truth that we cannot grow in holiness apart from the power of Christ that is ours through salvation.

None of us can kill sin on our own. Jesus doesn't call us to become holy *prior* to saving us by his grace, because we can't be holy *without* his grace. The only way to kill sin is through faith in Christ and the power of the Spirit. If we fail to remember this, we will try to turn mortification into a means of earning salvation—even though we are Christians. This reverses the order of the gospel. The good news of Jesus Christ is not "kill your sin and you will be accepted," but "God accepts you through faith in Christ alone, so pursue holiness in the power and joy of his acceptance."

Putting sin to death is the duty of every Christian, but no one can *become* a Christian through mortification. The only sins we can kill are the sins that have been forgiven through the shed blood of Jesus. Owen said, "There is no death of sin without the death of Christ."[4] To attempt to kill sin without Christ will only delude us and harden us further in our sins. *The first priority in dealing with sin is to look to the crucified Savior, Jesus Christ.*

In one of the most interesting stories in the Old Testament, the newly rescued people of Israel sinned by murmuring against God and his servant Moses. Their unprovoked sin was so evil that the Lord judged them by sending poisonous snakes into their camp. These "fiery serpents . . . bit the people, so that many people of Israel died." Then the people came to Moses, confessed their sin, and begged him to ask God to take the snakes away. Moses prayed for the people, and God gave him a strange command: he was to make a serpent from bronze and place it on a pole in the middle of the camp. Then, if someone had been bitten by a snake, he or she only had to look at the bronze snake in order to be healed. The simple act of gazing at the brazen serpent brought life and healing (see Numbers 21:4–9).

But more amazing is how Jesus used this story in the New Testament: "And as Moses lifted up the serpent in the wilderness, so must the Son of Man be lifted up, that whoever believes in him may have eternal life" (John 3:14–15).

The most important thing to understand in this first chapter is this: before you can kill sin, you have to look to the Lord who was lifted up on the cross for you. You cannot fight sin unless you have found rest in the inexhaustible sufficiency of the doing and dying of Jesus Christ in your place. You cannot mortify sin unless that sin has already been nailed to the cross of Christ. There is no death of sin without the death of Christ.

Examine and Apply

1.   Are you a genuine Christian? Do you have a relation-ship with God through faith in Jesus Christ that is characterized by a desire for holiness and a commit-ment to keep turning from sin? When did you first believe in Jesus?

2.   Is it news to you that sin isn't simply an external behavioral problem, but an internal problem of the heart? Think about your own struggles with sin. Have you been focused on modifying your behavior or changing your deepest desires, drives, and motives?

3.   Have you had unrealistic expectations for your Christian life? Have you been expecting to arrive at sinless perfection? How does learning about the ongoing conflict with indwelling sin affect you?

Personal Key —
Sin at war of sin
" be Always killing sin
or it will be preparing
to kill you "

Two

TOWARD LIFE OR DEATH

Why Sin Must Be Killed

Alone in the Utah wilderness, Aron Ralston was scaling a three-foot-wide slot canyon when he came upon some large boulders wedged into the opening. As he tried to scramble over them, one stone rolled free. Aron fell to the bottom of the slot, the 800-pound rock falling with him. As they landed, the boulder pinned his right hand to the wall.

He was out of sight, in a narrow crevice far below ground level, in a 500 square mile national park, and he could not free his hand. No one even knew he had gone climbing that day.

Ralston first tried to chip away at the boulder and cliff wall. It didn't work. His efforts to lift the boulder with his climbing gear also failed. A day passed with no progress, and then another.

On day three, Ralston's food and water ran out. He made a drastic decision: he would cut off his arm. But equipped with only a dull-bladed pocket knife, his initial attempts were unsuccessful.

On day four, Ralston determined to snap the bones in his arm, but couldn't bring himself to do it. On day five, he summoned the courage and performed the amputation.

First he snapped the radius, then the ulna, then the wrist. Ralston next applied a tourniquet and began cutting through skin, muscle, tissue, and nerve. The excruciating operation took an entire hellish hour. Finally free, Ralston still had to get out of the slot canyon, rappel down a sixty-five-foot wall, and begin the seventeen-mile hike to his car. Six hours later, after encountering a family of hikers who gave him water and alerted the authorities, he was rescued by a helicopter search team. Aron Ralston encountered one of the worst dilemmas any person could ever face. Passivity would lead to certain death. The only way to live was to take bold and decisive action. Ralston's decision to amputate his own hand was stark, gruesome, awful. But it was the right decision, the only rational choice under the circumstances. In fact, his decision echoes the kind of ruthless intention Jesus urges us to have when faced with the realities of sin, death, and hell.

> Whoever causes one of these little ones who believe in me to sin, it would be better for him if a great millstone were hung around his neck and he were thrown into the sea. [43] And if your hand causes you to sin, cut it off. It is better for you to enter life crippled than with two hands to go to hell, to the unquench-able fire. [45] And if your foot causes you to sin, cut it off. It is better for you to enter life lame than with two feet to be thrown into hell. [47] And if your eye causes

you to sin, tear it out. It is better for you to enter the kingdom of God with one eye than with two eyes to be thrown into hell, [48] "where their worm does not die and the fire is not quenched."(Mark 9:42–48)

Sin has placed the human race in a life and death predicament. Left unaddressed, sin always leads to hell. This is the unalterable principle of sin that Jesus explains to his disciples in this passage. Jesus warns against the deadly dangers of sin with the some of the starkest, most gruesome metaphors found in Scripture. He is exhorting his disciples to embrace the most costly sacrifices, the most radical refusals, and the most drastic measures in the fight against sin. He is calling us to a life of holy violence against sin.

Perhaps this raises some tensions in your mind. If you are not a believer (and I don't assume that all readers of this book will be), you might feel a tad confused or even a bit put off by such gruesome imagery. And if you are a Christian, you might read a passage like this, scratch your head, and think, "But I thought we were saved by grace alone, through faith alone. This stuff about 'cutting of a hand' and 'plucking out an eye' in order to avoid hell sounds more like salvation by works than salvation by grace!" Well, it would be dishonest for me or anyone else to pretend that Jesus' words are never shocking or offensive. But Jesus loves us enough to offend us with the truth. His warnings about hell do not contradict his consistent emphasis on God's love and mercy. They demonstrate, instead, just how deep that love is.

Nor is Jesus teaching that we are saved by works.

Jesus is speaking to us in terms of our fallen condition as rebellious human beings who live outside the reign of God's grace. And he is showing us how sin works and where it inevitably leads for all those who refuse to trust him for eternal life and entrance into the kingdom of God. Jesus is calling us to forsake our sins, no matter how dear to our hearts they are, and embrace instead his rule and reign as our true Lord and King. It is true that Jesus saves us by grace alone through faith in his saving work on the cross alone. As he later says to his disciples, he came "not to be served, but to serve, and to give his life as a ransom for many" (Mark 10:45). The ransom payment of his death effectively delivers all believers from the dreadful consequences of sin. No serving or working or striving on our part can earn us merit with God. But genuine faith in Christ's saving work always sets our feet on the narrow path of holiness and one of the means he uses to help us on this path are vivid warning signs that show us where sin leads for those who don't stay the path. A wise and careful driver on a winding mountain road will pay close attention to signs warning of steep ledges and falling rocks, and true faith will in like manner take note of the dangers of sin.

The Dangers of Sin

While sin cannot drag a true blood-washed believer in Jesus to hell, the basic lesson Jesus teaches in this passage is vital to the life of faith. Jesus' words still hold true: sin is out to ruin us, as badly as it can, dragging us as far away from God as it can, in any way that it can. Just as Aron Ralston didn't decide to sever his own arm until it was clear there was no other alternative, so we will not exert holy violence against our sins until we're convinced that they really are dangerous.

We often tolerate anger, avarice, and anxiety in our hearts because we don't see them the way Jesus does. We claim to believe that sin is an awful thing—after all, we're good Christians, aren't we?—yet we conveniently assume that in our special case our transgressions are really nothing more than minor offenses against overly rigid rules, like driving 5 mph over the speed limit. We treat sins like annoying warts—unpleasant, perhaps, but not threatening to a robust spiritual life. Christ, in contrast, considers them cancerous.

But everything in our hearts and in our culture tells us the opposite: that sin is no big deal. For many people outside the church this mindset is reinforced by the misguided belief that right and wrong are relative categories. (Although almost everyone, when pressed, will admit that there are some things such as rape, murder, and genocide which are absolutely wrong.) Those who are Christians, on the other hand, sometimes take sin too lightly because they wrongly view grace as a Get-Out-of-Jail-Free card. But the Scriptures counter both the false messages of our culture about right and wrong and the misguided logic of our fallen minds about sin and grace. Let's consider three specific dangers of sin.

Sin is deceitful. "But exhort one another every day, as long as it is called 'today,' that none of you may be hardened by the deceitfulness of sin" (Hebrews 3:13). Sin portrays itself as something other than what it really is. Sin comes to us in disguise. Sin looks satisfying, but hidden beneath the pleasing exterior are death and destruction. Sin is chocolate-covered poison. And, as this passage warns, sin's deceitfulness puts us in a precarious position. As leprosy damages the nerves, rendering a person incapable of feeling pain, thus tending toward disastrous injuries, so sin deadens our hearts to the warnings of conscience, tending toward the destruction of ourselves and others.

Sin is dehumanizing. Sin dismantles human relationships and corrupts the human soul. This is implicit in Scripture, which describes the new creation work of Christ and the Spirit as the restoration of human beings in the image of God. The less we bear the image of God due to the presence of sin, the less human we really are. We call some crimes *savage*, *beastly*, and *brutal* because they are so debased, so inhuman and inhumane, that we have to reach down for words to describe them. Sin dehumanizes us. And this is true for both believers and unbelievers. Sin, wherever it is present, always tends towards the deforming of the divine image within us, the dismantling of our relationships, and the distortion of our souls.

The dehumanizing effect of sin is vividly illustrated in C. S. Lewis's book *The Pilgrim's Regress.* In perhaps the most memorable scene in the book, the protagonist, John, discovers a group of disfigured and deformed men.

> [A]ll seemed to be suffering from some disease of a crumbling and disintegrating kind. . . . It was doubtful whether all the life that pulsated in their bodies was their own: and soon John was certain, for he saw what

seemed to be a growth on a man's arm slowly detach itself under his eyes and become a fat reddish creature, separable from the parent body.... Once he had seen that, his eyes were opened and he saw the same thing happening all round him, and the whole assembly was but a fountain of writhing and reptilian life quickening as he watched and sprouting out of the human forms.

Moving among these tormented men was a woman, a witch "dark, but beautiful," who carried a cup from which they longed to drink. Her name was Luxuria, the Latin word for self-indulgent sexual desire, one of the traditional seven deadly sins.

One young man looked healthy, though there was "an unpleasant suspicion about his fingers—something a little too supple for joints—a little independent of his other movements." As the witch moved near to him, "the hands shot out to the cup, and the man drew them back again: and the hands went crawling out for the cup a second time, and again the man wrenched them back, and turned his face away." The witch stood silently before him, saying nothing, "but only holding out the cup and smiling kindly on him with her dark eyes and her dark, red mouth." When he continued to refuse the drink, she began to walk away.

But at the first step she took, the young man gave a sob and his hands flew out and grabbed the cup and he buried his head in it: and when she took it from his lips, clung to it as a drowning man to a piece of wood. But at last he sank down in the swamp with a groan.

And the worms where there should have been fingers
were unmistakable.

Lewis's comment on this gruesome scene is telling:
"Lechery means not simply forbidden pleasure but loss of
the man's unity."[6] Sin divides our hearts, disintegrates our
souls, and disfigures the image of God within us. When
we choose to sin, we think it will make us feel happy,
alive, and whole. We are reluctant to reject any possible
satisfaction, no matter how illusory. But choosing sin will
never make us whole. Sin only makes us less human, less
ourselves, less what God intended us to be.

Sin is damning. Sin's greatest danger is its threat to
the eternal souls of the unsaved. As Scripture so often
warns, sin leads to death, judgment, and eternal punishment in hell. The doctrine of hell is not popular today,
but Jesus spoke unequivocally about it. His words in this
passage teach us three things about hell.

Hell is a fate worse than death. "Whoever causes
one of these little ones who believe in me to sin, it would
be better for him if a great millstone were hung around
his neck and he were thrown into the sea" (v 42). To be
thrown into the sea with a millstone around one's neck is a
death sentence. But Jesus says it would be better to receive
such a death sentence than the fate which awaits those
who cause a believing child to sin. So, whatever hell is, it is
worse than death.

Hell is the final destiny of those who refuse Jesus'
terms of discipleship and fail to enter into eternal life
in the kingdom of God. This is clear from the contrast

between hell and life in verses 43 and 45, and the contrast between hell and the kingdom of God in verse 47. There are only two possible destinies: life or death; the kingdom of God or destruction; heaven or hell.

Hell involves both painful and eternal punishment. This is evident from the phrase "unquenchable fire" in verse 43, as well as the vivid imagery of verse 48: "where their worm does not die and the fire is not quenched." This is a quotation from Isaiah 66:24, which describes God's future judgment of the wicked with an allusion to the Valley of Hinnom. The prophets of the Old Testament declared God's judgment against the Valley of Hinnom because that was where the idolatrous people of Israel sacrificed their children by fire to the god Molech. Eventually, the Valley of Hinnom (or *gehenna,* the Greek word for hell used in this passage) was equated with God's final judgment of the wicked, where the fires will never stop burning and the maggots will never stop feeding.

This imagery tells us something about the conditions of hell. *Externally*, fire burns and consumes, disintegrates and destroys, while the worm symbolizes the *internal* condition of the condemned person. The damned not only will be eternally consumed by the fires of God's unmitigated judgment, they will be everlastingly devoured by the gnawing pain of their sinful cravings and the torments of their self-condemning consciences. "Not only will the unbeliever be in hell, but hell will be in him, too."[7]

This is frightening imagery that should cause us to both weep and fear. Jesus uses these images to portray the severity of eternal judgment. To refuse his forgiveness, spurn his words, and disdain his claims is to choose for our eternal destiny unending punishment under the righteous judgment and wrath of God. Jesus doesn't spare us this knowledge any more than a good oncologist spares her patient the grim prognosis of cancer. But there is mercy in Jesus' words, for the cancer of sin that leads to eternal death can be removed.

Drastic Measures Required

Because Jesus understands the dangers of sin, he urges us to be ruthless with it in our lives. He says that we should cut off our hands, cut off our feet, and pluck out our eyes if these organs cause us to sin.

Some people have mistaken Jesus' hyperbole as a call for literal self-mutilation. But we can reject that interpretation with confidence because Jesus elsewhere makes it clear that our problem lies in the heart (e.g., Mark 7:20–23). Pulling out an eye won't cure a lust problem because adultery and sexual immorality proceed from the heart. No, Jesus is calling for mortification, not mutilation.

But this still sounds drastic, especially to modern people who prize personal autonomy and individual freedom. In fact, even some religious people react negatively to the idea that Jesus could be so severe in dealing with sin. Several years ago, a friend of mine preached a message on mortifying sin. After the sermon, a woman in the church told him that she didn't like the sermon and had no intention of applying it. He thought she must have misunderstood, so he began to clarify what he meant by mortification. But as he clarified, she confirmed that she *had*, in fact, understood him and would *not* be mortifying sin! "I'm not going to do that!" she said with finality. She left the church and began attending another church in the same town.

Her reaction wasn't that different from the typical response of an unbeliever who resists Jesus' moral demands because they seem overly restrictive. But these reactions underestimate the deadliness of sin. Sin, like a cancer, eats away at our hearts and souls, rendering us incapable of receiving God's love for us or loving him and others in return. Sin leads to hell in the same way that melanoma leads to death.

This is why Scripture insists that salvation involves not only *forgiveness for* sin but also *freedom from* sin. We are called to resist and renounce sin because sin is a kind of slavery, a slavery leading to death (see Romans 6:15–23). But Christ came to rescue us from slavery to sin and the death to which it leads. That's why both Jesus and Paul tell us to mortify it, to cut it off, to put it to death: "So then, brothers, we are debtors, not to the flesh, to live according to the flesh. For if you live according to the flesh you will die, but if by the Spirit you *put to death* the deeds of the body, you will live" (Romans 8:12-13).

This statement draws motivational force from the surrounding context. As believers, we are in Christ Jesus, and have therefore been delivered from condemnation and set free from the law of sin and death (Romans 8:1-3). We have also been indwelt by the Spirit of Christ (v 9), who will someday give life to our mortal bodies (v 11). So the call to mortify sin is framed by the reality of salvation from the condemnation of sin (in the past) and the confident expectation of resurrection life (in the future). These realities do not nullify the demand to mortify sin. No, the certainties of our past justification and our future glorification empower us for present sanctification. This is how grace empowers mortification. (We will return to this again in chapter six).

✈ **Holy Violence Against Sin**

The Bible is never casual toward sin. Rather, Scripture urges what the Puritans called a "holy violence" against sin in all its varied forms. What does this holy violence against sin look like? It begins with a wartime mentality, an Aron Ralston kind of ruthlessness toward evil, a mindset that takes biblical warnings and demands seriously. There are three specific forms this holy violence against sin should take in our lives.

We should be putting sin to death in all areas of our lives, not just some areas. This is one of the tests of our sincerity. Are we committed to obedience in all areas of life? Sometimes we are selective in mortifying sin. We kill most of our sins, but not all of them. We spare the respectable sins that most people overlook or the dark sins that dwell deep in our hearts. We quickly settle for partial obedience. Maybe you are ruthless in dealing with lust, but are you also seeking to mortify your anger problem? Ask the Spirit to examine your heart, to show you anything that grieves his heart or quenches his influence. Then set yourself to mortify all your sins, not only the obvious or easy ones.

We should give no opportunity to sin. "Make no provision for the flesh, to gratify its desires" (Romans

13:14). There are some things we must not do and some places we must not go if we are to guard ourselves against sin. For one of my friends, this means never drinking alcohol. For him, the temptation to drunkenness is too strong. For others, it means no unprotected time on the Internet, lest they fall into pornography. In order to apply this command, you have to study your heart and know your unique temptations.

__We should reject the first solicitations of sin.__ This means saying _no_ to temptation immediately. We must not pause to consider whether we will give in, for if we do our resolve will weaken. Eventually we will fall. Which fire is harder to extinguish, the flicker of a match or the blaze of a forest fire? Fires start small, then get bigger. "_Rise mightily against the first sign of sin. Do not allow it to gain the smallest ground._"[8]

The promises of grace and salvation made to sinners in Scripture are great. But they are promises made to those who believe _and_ repent. God's purpose is _not only to save us_ from the penalty of our sins _but to actually deliver us_ from sin's power and pollution. To be sure, this deliverance is a gradual process that takes place over time, amid many failures and setbacks. We are not yet fully redeemed. Sinful flesh still wages war against the soul. But though grace gives peace to sinners, it does not make peace with their sins. It rather calls us to arms and gives us the unceasing mandate of mortifying sin. Because turning from sin really is a matter of life and death.

Jesus tells us that it is better to lose a hand or an eye than for one's whole body to be thrown into hell. But on the cross, Jesus himself, body and soul, was "thrown into hell" for us. He absorbed the wrath we deserved in order to free us from both the curse and captivity of sin. Our only hope of turning *from* sin is in turning *to* Jesus, who became sin for us. The only reason we can wage war on sin with holy violence is because Christ himself suffered the violence of the cross for us. The only way to escape hell is to trust in the one who took hell in our place.

Examine and Apply

1. Do you find Jesus' words about dealing with sin shocking? Do you find them offensive?

2. Are you sufficiently aware of the dangers of sin? Do you have a healthy fear of God and eternal punishment? If you are a believer, have you developed an unhealthy Get-Out-of-Jail-Free card mentality about grace?

3. As you examine your life, do you see evidences that you have been *deceived* by sin?

4. Have you witnessed the *dehumanizing effects* of sin in your life and relationships?

5. Is your life characterized by holy violence against sin? Has it *ever* been characterized by holy violence against sin? Why did that end? How could it begin again?

6. Are there any sins you have left untouched? Are you frequently yielding to the solicitations of sin? Where in your life are you giving sin an opportunity?

Key App:
Holy violence — Verbal Repentance
to Another
+
Rejecting at first
Solitication

32

Three
THE MONSTER WITHIN

Understanding Indwelling Sin

"Deliver me from that evil man, myself."

This prayer, usually credited to Augustine of Hippo, strikes a chord in the echo chamber of my heart. But the chord is minor and turns sour. I find a strange, sorrowful comfort in the prayer, but it also forces me to face an awful reality about myself: *something inside me hates God.*

That's a shocking thing for a pastor to admit, but it's true—at least partly true. There is something in me that is anti-God, opposed to him in thought and intention, rebellious to the core.

But there is a contradictory affection coexisting with this corruption in the center of my being. There is a new me, a re-fashioned yet still-under-construction me that is being renovated in the image of Christ, a me that delights in God with unparalleled wonder. There are remnants of the old, miserable me: the monster within that insists on its own way, no matter the cost. But there is a new, humbled, and redeemed me that wants to walk in the will and ways of God. Something in me hates God even while I love him. I'm at war with myself.

I'm glad that no less a saint than Paul also experienced this disturbing dichotomy of desires. We can hear it in Romans 7, where Paul sets the goodness of God's holy law in stark contrast with "another law" that he finds hidden in his angst-ridden heart. His self-description reads like a conflicted journal entry from Dr. Jekyll and Mr. Hyde. But Paul doesn't have a first-century case of dissociative identity disorder. He is not schizophrenic. He is talking about his battle with a ruthless enemy that hides inside the hearts of all believers. He is talking about indwelling sin.

> For we know that the law is spiritual, but I am of the flesh, sold under sin. I do not understand my own actions. [15]For I do not do what I want, but I do the very thing I hate. [16]Now if I do what I do not want, I agree with the law, that it is good. [17]So now it is no longer I who do it, but sin that dwells within me. [18]For I know that nothing good dwells in me, that is, in my flesh. For I have the desire to do what is right, but not the ability to carry it out. [19]For I do not do the good I want, but the evil I do not want is what I keep on doing. [20]Now if I do what I do not want, it is no longer I who do it, but sin that dwells within me. [21]So I find it to be a law that when I want to do right, evil lies close at hand. [22]For I delight in the law of God, in my inner being, [23]but I see in my members another law waging war against the law of my mind and making me captive to the law of sin that dwells

in my members. ²⁴Wretched man that I am! Who will
deliver me from this body of death? ²⁵Thanks be to
God through Jesus Christ our Lord! So then, I myself
serve the law of God with my mind, but with my
flesh I serve the law of sin. (Romans 7:14–25)

The Law of Sin That Dwells Within

We do not simply do sinful acts. We have an inward
disposition to sin, a disposition that itself is sinful. Paul
experienced this, too; that is why he accounts for the
raging war of desires in his soul by twice attributing the
evil that confounds him to the "sin that dwells within me"
(vv 17, 20).

The images he employs to describe indwelling sin are
varied. In verse 23, he calls this propensity toward sin *a
law*: "But I see in my members another law waging war
against the law of my mind and making me captive to the
law of sin that dwells in my members."

In verse 25, Paul says that he serves the law of sin
with his *flesh*. By *flesh*, he doesn't mean his physical body,
but rather the fallen disposition within him that is both
anti-God and anti-good. We know the flesh is *anti-good*
because verse 18 says, "For I know that nothing good
dwells in me, that is, in my flesh." We know the flesh is
anti-God because Romans 8:7 says, "For the mind that is
set on the flesh is hostile to God, for it does not submit to
God's law; indeed, it cannot."

You see, there is something within us that is hostile
to God. Even as believers, we still have a complex of

thoughts and desires that don't like God or his ways. This aversion to God is the greatest source of ongoing grief in any believer's life. This is why Paul says: "Wretched man that I am! Who will deliver me from this body of death?" (Romans 7:24). In the words of Robert Robertson, the conflicted believer cries,

> Prone to wander, Lord, I feel it,
> Prone to leave the God I love [9]

Though Sin Is Present, It Has No Authority

Paul's words in Romans 7 have to be read in light of his teaching in Romans 6, and putting the two chapters together isn't as easy as you might think. Don't forget that even Peter admitted that Paul wrote some things that were hard to understand (Peter 3:16)!

In Romans 6, Paul says that believers must not continue in sin because they have already died to sin's power through their union with Christ in his death and resurrection. We are dead to sin. Therefore, we must not let it reign in our mortal bodies (Romans 6:11-12). Sin is no longer our master and we are no longer its slaves: therefore, we must not obey its demands (Romans 6:15-19). As Paul emphatically states in verse 14: *"Sin shall have no dominion over you."* Reading a statement like this could leave you with a reasonable question: If sin has no dominion over us, why does Paul say that we must not let it "reign"? Or, to put the question another way, if we really are dead to sin, why do we still struggle with it?

These are understandable questions about the complicated reality of our relationship to sin. Paul himself stretches the limits of language in his effort to describe how we do and do not relate to sin. At the risk of being a bit reductionistic, I think we can summarize it like this.

- In Romans 6, Paul says that we have died to the *authority* of sin. But in Romans 7 he reminds us that we are *not* dead to the *influence* of sin. Sin has no authority, but it is still present.
- In Romans 6 he says that we are not the slaves of sin. It does not master us and we should not live as though it does. But in Romans 7 he reminds us that we are still at war with sin.
- To put it all together in one sentence: *the bondage to sin is broken, but the conflict with sin continues.*

Now, consider a helpful, though imperfect, analogy. Imagine that an undercover spy is lurking in the White House administration plotting an act of terrorism against the United States. There is a huge difference between the relative positions of the President of the United States and the seditious mole. Both are *resident* in the White House, but only the *President* has legitimate executive authority. The mole works by deception, manipulation, and subterfuge. But he has no right to be there, no rightful rank in the chain of command.

In much the same way, sin is resident, not president, in the believer's heart. The dominion of sin has ended. Its authority to rule is removed, its stranglehold broken. It has influence, but no legitimate authority to rule over us. It is an insidious mole in the believer's heart that works through manipulation, deception, and subterfuge.

The Presence of Indwelling Sin Results In Ongoing Conflict

At every turn, sin uses its influence to oppose our will to obey the Lord. This is why Paul's inner dialogue in Romans 7 (especially vv 15 and 18 -20) sounds like Smeagol/Gollum arguing with himself in J.R.R. Tolkien's *The Lord of the Rings.*

The Scriptures testify that this experience of inward turmoil in the battle against sin is common for believers. Peter said, "Beloved, I urge you as sojourners and exiles to abstain from the passions of the flesh, which wage war against your soul" (1 Peter 2:11). Our flesh has passions that wage unrelenting guerrilla warfare against our souls. Our sinful dispositions and desires live in continual, subtle, malignant conflict with the desires of the Holy Spirit: "For the desires of the flesh are against the Spirit, and the desires of the Spirit are against the flesh, for these are opposed to each other, to keep you from doing the things you want to do" (Galatians 5:17).

We Need More Than God's Law to Change Us—We Need Grace

In the larger argument of his letter, Paul's central concern is to show that though God's law is good, it is insufficient to save us or change us. The law cannot justify (Romans 3:20). Neither can it sanctify. The power of sin, like the law of gravity, drags us down, even in our best efforts: "So I find it to be a law that when I want to do right, evil lies close at hand" (Romans 7:21). This prompts Paul's miserable confession in verse 24: "Wretched man that I am! Who will deliver me from this body of death?" Thankfully, there is an answer to Paul's question: "Thanks be to God through Jesus Christ our Lord!" (v 25a).

As Paul goes on to teach in the following verses, and as we'll learn later in this book, God does for us what the law cannot do. By sending his Son to die for us and his Spirit to live in us, he causes another law to kick in—a law that brings progressive freedom from this gravity of depravity, the down-drag of sin: "For the law of the Spirit of life has set you free in Christ Jesus from the law of sin and death" (Romans 8:2). The gravitational pull of sin is overcome by the aerodynamics of grace in the Father's gift of his Son and Spirit. As one author put it,

> "Run, John, run," the law demands,
> But gives me neither feet nor hands.
> Better news the Gospel brings,
> It bids me fly and gives me wings. [10]

Examine and Apply

1. Can you relate to Paul's experience of inner conflict? Does this comfort you or discourage you?

2. Sin is present, but has no authority. Is this true in your life? Are there any areas of life where you have yielded to sin as if it did have authority? Read

Why are you walking through this struggle w/?

through Romans 6 and underline all the reasons why Paul says sin does not have authority in the life of a believer.

3. Has your struggle against sin made you more desperate for God's grace?

Four

WITH MURDEROUS INTENT

How Sin Works in Our Souls

Call me a nerd, but I am a huge fan of *Star Wars*. I spent countless hours as a kid in intergalactic reverie with my Darth Vader, Luke Skywalker, and Han Solo action figures. George Lucas's space opera was (and is!) the perfect blend of drama, action, humor, and special effects. Few films have brought me more delight than the original *Star Wars* trilogy. In fact, if you were to ask Holly (my wife) what my favorite film of all time is, she would say, with zero hesitation, *The Empire Strikes Back*. And despite the stilted scripts and overblown CGI effects in the more recent prequels, I am still mesmerized every time I watch the evil Chancellor Palpatine seduce Anakin Skywalker to the dark side of the force in *Revenge of the Sith*.

The story of the young Jedi knight's temptation and fall resonates with me because it is not that different from the way sin tricks and tempts me. Palpatine knows exactly how to push Anakin's buttons. He seduces the knight by seizing on his passionate love for his bride and his compulsive fear of losing her; by undermining his trust in his true mentors and friends; and by clouding his mind with deceptive promises of power. In much the same way, indwelling sin seizes on my passions and fears, undermines my confidence in God and his Word, and clouds my head with a fog of shrewd lies and false promises.

The Bible vividly describes the bait-and-switch tactics of sin and temptation in James 1:14-15.

- Verse 14 exposes the *strategy of the flesh*. This is the bait. "Each person is tempted when he is lured and enticed by his own desire." From the context of the passage, it is obvious that this refers to sinful desire.
- Verse 15 summarizes the *sequence of sin*. Here we see the switch. "Desire when it has conceived gives birth to sin, and sin when it is fully grown brings forth death."

Mixing the metaphors of an angler luring fish to their death, and the process of gestation and growth from conception to birth to maturity, James provides us with a frightful description of sin's lethal goal and the insidious steps it takes in pursuit of our destruction. Aided by the allurements of this evil age and the crafty schemes of our enemy the Devil, sin conspires against God and the soul. This unholy trinity of world, flesh, and Devil collude with one purpose in mind: death.

Let's look at how the flesh:

- deceives the mind and entices the affections,
- with the goal of winning the cooperation of our will, thus conceiving sin,
- so that sin can begin its march of murderous intent.

Sinful Desire Deceives the Mind

The mind is that faculty of the human personality that thinks and discerns. The duty of the mind in relation to sin is to discern its evil nature and its danger to the soul. And that's why temptation usually begins with deception.

As any angler knows, a good catch depends on a cleverly disguised hook. Like the shady government agencies in *The X-Files* (yeah, I'm a sci-fi junkie), the *modus operandi* of indwelling sin is "Deceive. Inveigle. Obfuscate." If the mind can be tricked into thinking that sin promises more happiness than can be gained through righteousness, or is less dangerous than it really is, the affections are far more likely to bite. That's why the flesh first targets the mind.

Think of any high-tech heist story. The only way a troupe of sophisticated thieves can pull off an elaborate robbery is to neutralize the surveillance system. If the alarms are disabled, the images on the video monitors falsified, and the security guards distracted, the crooks have a much better chance of breaking in, grabbing the loot, and disappearing without notice.

One of the functions of the mind is to serve as the surveillance system for the soul. So, for sin to ply its trade on us, it first has to neutralize the mind. And it does this in several ways:

Sinful desire exploits our natural weaknesses and limitations. Just as Palpatine used Anakin's love for his bride against him, we all have *particular* weaknesses and limitations that sin will seek to exploit. But we also share *universal* tendencies toward weakness.

Twelve-step programs, for example, often use the acronym H.A.L.T. to warn recovering addicts against relapses, because there are certain times when anyone is more vulnerable to temptation — when we are Hungry, Angry, Lonely, or Tired. The sin within us also knows this and seizes every possible advantage these conditions provide.

Sinful desire tricks the mind into thinking that sinning is no big deal. Through subtle insinuations and crafty arguments, the flesh tries to influence our perception of sin and its dynamics. Its goal is that we would increasingly:

- excuse our own motives for sin
- overestimate the pleasure we expect sin to deliver
- underestimate the pain and consequences we expect sin to produce

Sinful desire leads us to abuse God's grace. The flesh suggests that since God has promised to pardon our sins, we need not worry about them. Or it suggests that we can take grace for granted, that we should claim for ourselves greater liberty than Scripture allows, or that there is no need for us to take severe, radical measures against sin.

In its zeal to deceive, indwelling sin will even quote

Scripture to us, albeit selectively. For example, it may remind us that, "If anyone does sin, we have an advocate with the Father, Jesus Christ the righteous" (1 John 2:1b). Yet it will cloak from our memories the phrase that the author was careful to place immediately prior: "I am writing these things to you *so that you may not sin*" (v 1a).

Sin employs twisted logic to lead us away from grace. It wants us to behave like a cancer patient who is given the promise of recovery by his attending physician, but then chooses to forgo surgery, chemotherapy, and radiation, not realizing that the promised recovery is contingent on following the doctor's orders!

Sin also assaults the mind by disassembling the components of theological truths from one another. It tries to separate justification (right standing before God) from progressive sanctification (increasing holiness in our actual lives). It seeks to highlight our pardon from guilt, yet obscure our freedom from slavery. It wants the removal of sin's curse, without the cleansing of sin's stain.

Through deception and distraction, sinful desire seeks to make the mind more open to temptation. When it succeeds, the affections will always follow.

Sinful Desire Entices the Affections

If the mind is the discerning faculty of the soul, the affections are the embracing faculty of the soul. With the affections we love and hate, rejoice and recoil, delight and detest. The process of temptation usually starts with deceiving the mind, then progresses by enticing the affections. When your affec-

tions are enticed, you begin to cherish iniquity in your heart.
Though you haven't swallowed the sugar-coated morsel of
poison quite yet, you are now rolling it around with your
tongue, enjoying the taste.

Dietrich Bonhoeffer, in his classic study of temptation, provides an insightful description of the process:

> In our members there is a slumbering inclination
> toward desire, which is both sudden and fierce. With
> irresistible power desire seizes master over the flesh.
> All at once a secret, smouldering fire is kindled. The
> flesh burns and is in flames. It makes no difference
> whether it is sexual desire, or ambition, or vanity,
> or desire for revenge, or love of fame and power,
> or greed for money ... Joy in God is in course of
> being extinguished in us as we seek all our joy in the
> creature. At this moment God is quite unreal to us, he
> loses all reality, and only desire for the creature is real
> ... The powers of clear discrimination and of decision
> are taken from us. The questions present themselves:
> "Is what the flesh desires really sin in this case?" "Is it
> really not permitted to me, yes – expected of me, now,
> here, in my particular situation, to appease desire?"
> ... It is here that everything within me rises up against
> the Word of God. [11]

How do you know if you've been seduced? Ask the
following diagnostic questions:

**Do I find myself frequently thinking about
something sinful? Is my imagination possessed by**

<u>some sinful object, attraction, or desire?</u> Peter speaks of those whose eyes are full of adultery and cannot cease from sin (2 Peter 2:14). John warns us against the lusts or desires of the eyes (1 John 2:16). Remember that Eve was enticed to sin because of what she first *saw*.

<u>Do I dwell on sin with private pleasure? When I think about some temptation to sin, do I taste its sweetness with the tongue of my soul?</u> It may be an illicit sexual desire, a lust for getting even, or some secret self-indulgence. It may even be something that you would never dream of *actually* doing. But the *thought* of it still gives you pleasure.

<u>Do I rationalize? Do I find myself arguing against conviction?</u> "It's just a little sin." "No one is perfect." "God will forgive me." "I won't go too far." "I'll give this up soon." This is the language of sin in a deceived and enticed heart. If you are willing to be tempted by sin, to fondly consider its proposals, to carry on a peaceful courtship with the flesh, you have already become unfaithful in your heart to Christ, your Bridegroom. It is to such hearts that Paul says: "I feel a divine jealousy for you, since I betrothed you to one husband, to present you as a pure virgin to Christ. But I am afraid that as the serpent deceived Eve by his cunning, your thoughts will be led astray from a sincere and pure devotion to Christ" (2 Corinthians 11:2–3).

Sinful Desire Conquers the Will

With the mind deceived and the affections enticed, the will quickly consents to sin. Unless God intervenes with grace, conceived desires give birth to actual sins. We commit sin intentionally. Our eyes are peeled for opportunities to fulfill our ungodly cravings.

Sin secures its capture of the will in two basic ways.

Suddenly and violently. Sometimes sin comes with a sudden temptation, presenting something evil as good. It may appear with a violent provocation, in the form of strong, forceful temptations. With its unexpected timing, such temptation catches you off-guard, and you yield. Like a boat without ballast, the soul's resistance to sin is easily blown over by a single gust of strong wind.

Frequently and often imperceptibly. Or, perhaps the flesh gains its victory through a number of small, imperceptible steps. Through many smaller compromises, you eventually commit a sin that at one time you would never have dreamed of. At other times, the will is won over by frequent solicitations. The temptations are presented again and again, day after day, until the will is eventually worn down and surrenders to seduction.

It is in the nature of sin to pursue its course little by little, to the very end. Every intentional indulgence of lust would become adultery if it could. Greedy desires are content with nothing less than *having*, even if it means stealing to get. That look that *could* kill *would* kill – if it had its way. And a bitter heart, seething in its desire for revenge, will eventually find a way to get its pound of flesh. This is the DNA of sin. It is an anti-God, anti-good mindset. That is why a sinful desire once conceived will give birth to a sinful action – if it gets the opportunity.

By God's grace, such desires often do *not* get the

opportunity. Sometimes this is because God's providence prevents the flesh from accomplishing its design. The woman you flirt with rebuffs your advances. You are ready with an angry retort, but the phone rings before you get it out. For the believer, God always aborts sin before it reaches its final end in eternal destruction and death. He often does this through arresting our attention with warnings, and sometimes, when necessary, by chastening us with afflictions and trials (Hebrews 12:5-11). Even when our wills temporarily consent to sin, there is resistance from the Holy Spirit and the principle of grace within us.

When I watch Anakin Skywalker's descent to the dark side, I want to leap into the film, grab him by the shoulders, and shout, "Don't you realize what you're doing? You're buying into a lie! Palpatine is not your friend – he's an evil lord of darkness. Listening to him is going to destroy your life and the lives of those you love!"

I know. It's just a movie.

But then I remember that I am in a *real* cosmic war, a struggle between good and evil, light and darkness. The stakes are much higher in this struggle. But the good side is also infinitely stronger!

Scripture tells us that Jesus also faced temptation. "For we do not have a high priest who is unable to sympathize with our weaknesses, but one who in every respect has been tempted as we are, yet without sin" (Hebrews 4:15). "For because he himself has suffered when tempted, he is able to help those who are being tempted" (Hebrews 2:18). He faced the full gamut of temptation without ever being drawn into sin. This means that he fully understands our weaknesses, so he is able to strengthen us to stand when we are tempted. But he helped us most when he fought and won the decisive battle against evil for us. The first Adam faced temptation in the ideal conditions of a garden and gave in. But the Second Adam has faced and resisted temptation in the harsh wilderness of our fallen world. Then, in his triumph he crushed the serpent's head. Now he equips us to fight temptation with his Word and Spirit under the banner of his cross. We are on the winning side!

Examine and Apply

1. How has your mind been lured away by the trickery of sin? Do you ever use God's grace and forgiveness as an excuse for continuing in sin?

2. Does sin have a hold on your affections? Do you find yourself frequently thinking about something sinful? Is your imagination possessed by some sinful object, attraction, or desire?

3. Examine your life over the past thirty days. Where has sin conquered your will? How has God's grace intervened to prevent you from descending further into a sinful pattern of life? Talk to a pastor or friend about your struggles.

Five
SOUL SURGERY

Preparing for Mortification

When John Duncan, a nineteenth-century Scottish minister and professor of Hebrew, assigned his students a reading project, he added this stark warning: "But prepare for the knife!"[12] The book he had assigned was John Owen's *Indwelling Sin in Believers.* Duncan knew this to be the heart-searching work of a skilled soul surgeon who would spare no sin as he applied the scalpel of Scripture. Indeed, in this well-known passage from the book of Hebrews, the Bible's self-description makes the surgical metaphor explicit.

> For the word of God is living and active, sharper than any two-edged sword, piercing to the division of soul and of spirit, of joints and of marrow, and discerning the thoughts and intentions of the heart. And no creature is hidden from his sight, but all are naked and exposed to the eyes of him to whom we must give account. (Hebrews 4:12–13)

The Greek word for "sword" in this passage sometimes referred to a surgeon's knife, and the thrust of the passage is that this knife pierces so we might gain discernment at the deepest spiritual level. This chapter, therefore, is about diagnosis — allowing the Word of God to perform exploratory surgery on our souls. In this way, we can truly discern the areas of sin that need mortification.

Almost no one enters surgery lightly, not even exploratory surgery. Even the simplest procedure should warrant caution and care from all concerned. Cutting into the physical body is no trivial affair, and neither is surgery of the soul. Owen is a helpful guide in this regard, especially in our sound-bite age, in which we're tempted to oversimplify what is really complex. In his book on mortification, Owen provides a lengthy series of "preparatory directions to mortifying sin." These directions are aimed not at the work of mortification itself, but at helping his readers diagnose their spiritual condition and properly frame their hearts for the duty of killing sin. Owen provides nine of these directions (with numerous sub-headings!), but we can summarize his guidance in three points.

- Diagnose your sin accurately
- Cultivate a right view of both God and self
- Don't presume peace, but wait on the Lord

Diagnose Your Sin Accurately

Diagnosis always precedes cure, so the first prerequisite to dealing with sin is to understand the depth of the problem. We can begin by examining ourselves for the symptoms of unmortified sins. Select an area of your life where you

suspect sin is at work, and ask yourself the following
questions:

- *Is this sin habitual?*
- *Do I tend to apply "cheap grace" to my sin, assuring
  myself of forgiveness, even when I have not repented
  (turned from) the sin?*
- *Do I find myself frequently yielding to temptation?*
- *Is my predominant motivation in fighting this sin my
  fear of the likely consequences if I were to be found out?*
- *Has God already begun to chasten me for this sin?*

If your answer to any of these questions is yes, you
have killing work to do. Your sin is unmortified.

Such a diagnostic exercise will make us feel worse, not
better. But this can be a good thing. As Owen writes, you
need to "get a clear and abiding sense upon your mind
and conscience of the guilt, danger, and evil of the sin
with which you are troubled."[13] But getting this clear and
abiding sense of sin is difficult, because sin blows smoke
in our eyes to prevent us from seeing its true features.
"The heart is deceitful above all things, and desperately
sick; who can understand it?" (Jeremiah 17:9).

Our hearts get distracted by disordered desires,
befuddled by false promises, and confused by convo-
luted logic that lessens our sense of guilt. We may even
reason that we shouldn't feel guilty, since we are saved
and forgiven. When this kind of twisted reasoning sweeps
in, we should remember that Scripture itself condemns
those who "pervert the grace of our God into a license for

immorality" (Jude 1:4, NIV). If we are Christians — those truly united to Christ — then we have died to sin and have been raised *for a particular purpose*: to walk in newness of life (Romans 6:1-4). For a Christian to see grace as a license to sin is thus the height of presumption. It is to sin not only against God's law, but against his mercy.

We also need to see that unmortified sin is a grave danger. Even Christians can become hardened by the deceitfulness of sin (Hebrews 3:12-13). To continue in sin is also to come under the chastening hand of God. While all the afflictions God sends his children are sent in mercy, such mercy can be severe (Hebrews 12:5-11). Further, sin wearies the heart of God (Isaiah 43:25), grieves the Holy Spirit (Ephesians 4:30), and renders us useless (Matthew 5:13) and even harmful (2 Samuel 12:9-15) to others. And if we keep on sinning with no repentance, what assurances do we have that we are genuine Christians at all? "No one who abides in him keeps on sinning; no one who keeps on sinning has either seen him or known him" (1 John 3:6).

We need to meditate on the true nature of sin until we load our consciences with its guilt and inflame our hearts with a longing to be liberated from its hold on our lives. As long as we can either justify our failures with rationalizations and excuses, or rest content with unrepentant sin and low levels of holiness, we will not be deeply determined to give sin the death blow.

It is also helpful to ask whether our temperaments, circumstances, or past experiences make us more prone to particular sins or more vulnerable in particular situations. Human beings are complicated and our sin patterns are enmeshed in all of our psychological, circumstantial, and relational complexity. Vast labyrinths of subconscious idiosyncrasies, inclinations, and inadequacies are concealed under the surface of our thoughts. These do not excuse our sins in the least, but they do make it easier for Satan to get an advantage over us. As the Spirit uses his Word and the insight of others to give you a deeper understanding of yourself, turn your growing self-awareness to your advantage by devising new strategies for guarding your heart in its particular weaknesses and temptations.

Cultivate a Right View of God and Self

The second step in this process of exploratory soul surgery is to cultivate a right view of both God and self. We need a right view of God because "the fear of the LORD is the beginning of wisdom, and the knowledge of the Holy One is insight" (Proverbs 9:10). We also need a right view of ourselves in order to humble us and help us apply the gospel to our particular needs. But as John Calvin observed, "Man never achieves a clear knowledge of himself unless he has first looked upon God's face, and then descends from contemplating him to scrutinize himself."[14]

To cultivate this double-knowledge, begin by meditating on the greatness and majesty of God as he is revealed in Scripture. Consider his glorious attributes.

Eternal. God is without beginning or end: "Before the mountains were brought forth, or ever you had formed the earth and the world, from everlasting to everlasting you are God" (Psalms 90:2).

Self-sufficient. God is dependent on no one and nothing else for his life, being, happiness, and joy: "The God who made the world and everything in it, being Lord of heaven and earth, does not live in temples made by man, nor is he served by human hands, as though he needed anything, since he himself gives to all mankind life and breath and everything" (Acts 17:24–25).

Omnipotent, omnipresent, omniscient. God has *all power*, is *present everywhere*, and *knows everything*. As someone once quipped, "Did it ever occur to you that nothing ever occurred to God?" He simply knows, and always has known, all there is to know: "Great is our Lord, and abundant in power; his understanding is beyond measure" (Psalms 147:5).

Sovereign. God rules at all times and over all things in heaven and earth. "The Lord has established his throne in the heavens, and his kingdom rules over all" (Psalms 103:19).

> His dominion is an everlasting dominion, and his kingdom endures from generation to generation; all the inhabitants of the earth are accounted as nothing, and he does according to his will among the host of heaven and among the inhabitants of the earth; and none can stay his hand or say to him, "What have you done?" (Daniel 4:34b–35)

Holy. God is also *holy*: "And the four living creatures, each of them with six wings, are full of eyes all around and within, and day and night they never cease to say, 'Holy,

holy, holy, is the Lord God Almighty, who was and is and is to come!'" (Revelation 4:8).

On and on we could go, filling page after page with these glorious ascriptions of the character of our almighty God, who is gracious *and* righteous, merciful *and* just.

Of course, the bare knowledge of God's character is one thing. To feel the gravity of the reality of his majesty is another. In the scriptural accounts, people who had visions of God fell on their faces in terror-stricken awe, adoration, and fear. Isaiah saw God in his resplendent holiness and cried, "Woe is me! For I am lost; for I am a man of unclean lips, and I dwell in the midst of a people of unclean lips; for my eyes have seen the King, the Lord of hosts!" (Isaiah 6:5). Moses, Job, Habakkuk, and John had similar experiences.

While we may not have visions like those of Isaiah and Job, we still have reason to fear and love God infinitely more than we do. The created world testifies of God's power and attributes; and we've been given the very words of God in holy Scripture, his supreme self-revelation in his Son, and the ministry of the Holy Spirit convicting us of sin, righteousness, and judgment (Psalms 19:1, 2 Timothy 3:16, Hebrews 1:1-2, John 16:7-11). Our problem is not lack knowledge or experience. It's that we've not allowed God's revelation to rest with proper weight on our hearts.

Here's the point: only when we see God as he really is will we see ourselves as we really are. This will make us loathe our sins. Kris Lundgaard compares this experience to a painful bone-marrow transplant, where the old, cancerous marrow is destroyed by radiation, then replaced with new, healthy marrow.

> God's terrible majesty is radiation. It X-rays a soul and shows that it's gorged with sin....God's radiating majesty kills the rotten marrow of sin and replaces it with humility. A heart humbled by God's terrible majesty can begin its recovery and grow strong. Sin can't thrive in a humble heart. [15]

Don't Presume Peace, but Wait on the Lord

Finally, we should not presume to give ourselves peace when dealing with our sins. It is all too easy for us to settle for a self-generated assurance, rather than waiting for the assurance of the Spirit. We must be careful lest we deceive ourselves by healing our wounds lightly, saying "'Peace, peace,' when there is no peace" (Jeremiah 6:14). Providing ourselves this kind of illusory peace and assurance of pardon is like a cancer patient presumptuously giving herself a clean bill of health. It is both safer and wiser to wait on an informed medical opinion.

So, what's the difference? How do we know whether we are giving ourselves a false assurance rather than receiving true peace from the Spirit of Christ? Owen suggested several tests by which to discern the difference. I'll summarize them for you in a series of questions.

Does your peace inspire anything less than hatred for your sins? "The fear of the LORD is the hatred of evil" (Proverbs 8:13a). Again, remember the examples of the saints in Scripture. When they saw God, they loathed their sins. Do you loathe yours?

Is your peace rooted in logic alone, thus failing to sweeten your heart with rest and contentment in Christ? God wants not only to deal with our sins, but to lead us into fellowship and communion with himself. When we've really tasted his grace and mercy, our souls will be satisfied and cry, "Whom have I in heaven but you? And there is nothing on earth that I desire besides you" (Psalms 73:25). If this soul-satisfaction is missing you will eventually go back to your sin. It is not truly mortified.

Is your peace superficial, dealing only with the fruits (sinful behaviors), rather than roots (sinful motives)? God lays his axe to the root of the tree (Matthew 3:10). His Word searches the thoughts and motives of the heart. Genuine repentance always deals with heart-sins, not just bad behavior.

Does your peace focus on only one sin, while leaving the others untouched? When the Holy Spirit is working, he doesn't do conviction cafeteria-style. Of course, we're never *fully* aware of *all* our sins. But if you are picking and choosing which sins to turn from, while leaving other known sins untouched, your repentance is incomplete.

Does your peace lead to greater humility before God? The repentant and forgiven heart is also a broken heart. No one who has experienced God's forgiveness feels worthy of it. If you have been pardoned by his grace, you won't take it lightly.

God's Word pierces our souls and exposes our sinful

hearts to the gaze a holy God. But we need more than to be pierced by the Word, we also the need the Word to be pierced for us. And he was. Scripture tells us that Jesus, the Word made flesh, was "pierced for our transgressions [and] crushed for our iniquities" (Isaiah 53:5, NIV). We can willingly submit ourselves to God's gaze because Jesus was shamefully exposed in our place on the cross. The reason we can endure the painful process of exploratory soul surgery is because we know that God's sharp, surgical Word will not only wound our hearts, but also heal us and make us whole.

Examine and Apply

1. Take a written inventory of your sins. Write about them in detail, giving special attention to the symptoms of unmortified sin:
   - Is your sin habitual?
   - Do you rationalize your disobedience?
   - Do you claim forgiveness without repentance?
   - Do you frequently yield to temptation?
   - Are you more motivated by fear of consequences than genuine hatred for the sin itself?
2. Meditate on the greatness and majesty of God. For help, try reading Psalm 145 aloud. Pay attention to the various declarations it makes about God's character.
3. What are some of the ways you've given yourself peace and assurance, rather than waiting on the Lord?

Six

TRANSFORMING GRACE

The Power of the Gospel

Lust was eating my lunch.

I was a teenager and a fairly new Christian. My parents were godly, this was prior to the Internet, and I wasn't yet allowed to date, so my exposure to temptation was relatively limited. Yet with my hormones howling like a hurricane, normal curiosity had combined with sinful cravings to lead me into wicked thoughts and habits.

In the preceding months, however, God's Spirit had begun to convict me deeply of my sin and conceive in my soul an insatiable appetite for Christ and holiness. My competing passions—for sexual gratification and progressive sanctification—meant one thing: conflict. I was at war with myself. Unfortunately, my tactics often relied on legalism. I was pursuing holiness primarily by works, not grace.

One month, for example, I vowed to fast from breakfast and lunch every time I succumbed to a particular temptation. It seemed like a good plan, one that would surely break the neck of lust and gain me victory once and for all. But the discipline quickly wore thin, especially when I found myself fasting two meals in a row for the third day in a single week. At that point lust was eating my lunch *and* my breakfast.

I was glad I hadn't made a lifetime vow! My attempts to fight were not working very well. My resistance felt more like bondage than freedom.

Since then, I've come to realize that at least three elements were missing from my battle plan.

> 1)Although I had trusted in Christ, I lacked a deep grasp of the transforming power of my union with Christ.
> 2) I was driven by guilt, not joy. I needed a deeper satisfaction, a new affection, to expel my affections for sin.
> 3) My focus was more on sin avoidance than on growing in Christlike character. I needed to learn the practical power of replacing sin with grace.

Scripture instructs us in proper battle tactics in Colossians 3:1-17.

> If then you have been raised with Christ, seek the things that are above, where Christ is, seated at the right hand of God. ²Set your minds on things that are above, not on things that are on earth. ³For you have died, and your life is hidden with Christ in God. ⁴When Christ who is your life appears, then

you also will appear with him in glory. [5]Put to death therefore what is earthly in you: sexual immorality, impurity, passion, evil desire, and covetousness, which is idolatry. [6]On account of these the wrath of God is coming. [7]In these you too once walked, when you were living in them. [8]But now you must put them all away: anger, wrath, malice, slander, and obscene talk from your mouth. [9]Do not lie to one another, seeing that you have put off the old self with its practices [10]and have put on the new self, which is being renewed in knowledge after the image of its creator. [11]Here there is not Greek and Jew, circumcised and uncircumcised, barbarian, Scythian, slave, free; but Christ is all, and in all. [12]Put on then, as God's chosen ones, holy and beloved, compassionate hearts, kindness, humility, meekness, and patience, [13]bearing with one another and, if one has a complaint against another, forgiving each other; as the Lord has forgiven you, so you also must forgive. [14]And above all these put on love, which binds everything together in perfect harmony. [15]And let the peace of Christ rule in your hearts, to which indeed you were called in one body. And be thankful. [16]Let the word of Christ dwell in you richly, teaching and admonishing one another in all wisdom, singing psalms and hymns and spiritual songs, with thankfulness in your hearts to God. [17]And whatever you do, in word or deed, do everything in the name of the Lord Jesus, giving thanks to God the Father through him.

While verse 5 commands us to kill sin, in the surrounding verses we learn how the grace of the gospel empowers us to obey that command. In this chapter, I want to highlight three ways the gospel empowers holiness:

- The *transforming* power of union with Christ
- The *expulsive* power of a new affection
- The *practical* power of replacing sin with grace

The Transforming Power of Union with Christ

Paul commands us to kill sin, but it's vital for us to notice that *he doesn't start there*. In his writings, Paul usually takes his time in getting to moral imperatives about how to live, and the letter to the Colossians is no exception.

In the first two chapters, he exults in the *supremacy of Christ* over all things and the *sufficiency of Christ* alone to give us all that we need. Chapter three begins by calling us to remember our *position in Christ*, the first three verses highlighting our union with Christ and reminding us that in him we have a new history, total security, and a glorious destiny. The truth of what Jesus has done has radically changed our past, present, and future.

<u>A new history: we have been raised with Christ.</u> "If then you have been raised with Christ, seek the things that are above, where Christ is, seated at the right hand of God" (v 1). John Owen said that Christ "lived for us, he died for us; *he was ours* in all he did, in all he suffered."[16] That's the focus of this passage. When Christ was raised from

the dead, we were raised with him. When he was seated at God's right hand, we were seated with him. Because of our union with Christ, we participate in all of his triumph. His history counts as ours. Because we are in him, all that is true for him is also true for us. No matter where we are in our progressive sanctification, we fight from a position of victory. We have already been raised with Christ!

Jeremy Taylor captured the power of the believer's union with Christ in this prayer: "Grant, O Lord, that in your wounds I may find my safety, in your stripes my cure, in your pain my peace, in your cross my victory, in your resurrection my triumph, and a crown of righteousness in the glories of your eternal kingdom."[17]

Total security: our lives are hidden with Christ in God. "For you have died, and your life is hidden with Christ in God" (v 3). We are joined to God through Christ. We are in union with him, participants in his life. We have already died in him and our lives are now hidden in his. Union with Christ is not something we are climbing toward, one rung of obedience at a time. It is already ours! This means that we are safe and secure. As Jesus said of his sheep: "I give them eternal life, and they will never perish, and no one will snatch them out of my hand. My Father, who has given them to me, is greater than all, and no one is able to snatch them out of the Father's hand" (John 10:28–29).

A glorious destiny: we will appear with Christ in glory. "When Christ who is your life appears, then you also will appear with him in glory" (v 4). The day is coming when Jesus will return, not in weakness but in power. And you and I will appear with him. We will conquer with him and inherit all that he inherits. We will rule at his side, as his loyal subjects and glorified fellow heirs. This is most glorious of all, because it tells us the end of our story. We will be perfect! "But our citizenship is in heaven, and from it we await a Savior, the Lord Jesus Christ, who will transform our lowly body to be like his glorious body, by the power that enables him even to subject all things to himself" Philippians 3:20–21).

There is liberating gospel logic to Paul's words. He is saying, in effect, that what is true of Jesus is now true of us. His past is our past. His present is our present. His future is our future. We can hear this logic of our union with Christ in Charles Wesley's famous hymn, "Christ the Lord Is Risen Today." One verse goes like this:

> Soar we now where Christ hath led,
> Following our exalted Head
> Made like Him, like Him we rise
> Ours the cross, the grave, the skies.[18]

You are secure in him. Live in light of that reality!

The Expulsive Power of a New Affection

What motivates you in the pursuit of holiness? Guilt? Fear? Or do you sometimes feel that you are lacking sufficient motivation altogether? If we're honest, we have to admit that our motives for dealing with sin and pursuing holiness are all too often inappropriate or inadequate.

What is missing?

Colossians 3 supplies the answer. Look at verse 2: "Set your mind on things that are above, not on things that are on earth." This command embraces more than mental activity. The word *mind* used here encompasses both the intellect and the affections of the heart. Paul is calling for nothing less than a total reorientation of the will by the power of the grace we have in Christ. Only such a transformation will result in a life of holiness. As Thomas Chalmers said, "The only way to dispossess [the heart] of an old affection is by the expulsive power of a new one."[19]

What does Paul mean by "things that are above"? Look at verse 3: "For you have died, and your life is hidden with Christ in God." We are to set our affections on things above because that is where Christ is, and we are joined to him.

Our affections, then, are to be set on Christ himself. We are empowered for holiness when we fill our minds and hearts with the glories of who Jesus is, what he has done for us, and all that he has purchased for us. Only when we cultivate this kind of mindset will we discover what Chalmers called "the expulsive power of a new affection."

The best biblical illustration of this principle comes from the life of Moses. In Hebrews 11, we are told that Moses preferred "to be mistreated with the people of God than to enjoy the fleeting pleasures of sin ... [and] considered the reproach of Christ greater wealth than the treasures of Egypt" (vv 25–26). What was the source of Moses' strength? What was it about his faith that enabled him to make such difficult choices? The text answers: "He was looking to the reward … [and] he endured as seeing him who is invisible" (vv 26–27). Moses' vision of God promised more satisfaction and greater reward than anything he would leave behind in Egypt. The power of God's promises liberated Moses from the inferior pleasures he left behind.

Greek mythology tells the fascinating story of Ulysses and his perilous journey home following the Trojan War.[20] Among the dangers Ulysses and his crew faced were the alluring Sirens. The Sirens were beautiful, dangerous bird-women, who lured sailors to shipwreck and death through their beguiling beauty, enticing voices, and enchanting songs. Desiring to hear them sing, yet leery of their seductive power, Ulysses filled the ears of his fellow sailors with wax and had himself lashed to the mast of the ship so that he could hear the Sirens' voices without succumbing to their mesmerizing music. Had it not been for the ropes, Ulysses would have perished.

But another story is told about the Sirens, this one involving Jason, leader of the Argonauts. Like Ulysses, he too faced the alluring beauty and enticing music of the Sirens. But his strategy didn't involve wax or ropes. Instead, Jason brought Orpheus, a musician so talented that he could tame beasts and move mountains. The more alluring music of Orpheus broke the spell of the Sirens, so that Jason and the Argonauts were unmoved by their enchantments.

Some people try to fight sin by metaphorically filling their ears with wax or strapping themselves to the mast with the ropes of external rules and regulations. But their hearts are still captivated by the Siren song of sinful pleasure. The gospel commends a better way: the expulsive power of a new affection. By setting our hearts on Christ, we can be captivated by a sweeter, more satisfying song. As Matthew Henry wrote, "The joy of the Lord will arm us against the assaults of our spiritual enemies and put our mouths out of taste for those pleasures with which the tempter baits his hooks."[21]

The Practical Power of Replacing Sin with Grace

Mortifying sin is like weeding a garden. Left to itself, a garden will become overgrown with weeds, choking out the good plants. Likewise, a person who doesn't put sin to death finds his heart so overgrown with sin that the comfort and joy of walking with Christ is choked out. But there is more to growing a healthy garden than weeding it. Good seeds must be planted, watered, and fertilized! Then God must give the growth. So it is in a life of holiness: we must weed out sin *and* cultivate the graces of the Spirit in our lives.

Putting off and putting on. This is easy to see in Colossians 3. In verses 5–9, Paul commands us to put sin to death. Verse 5 begins, "Put to death therefore what is earthly in you." By "earthly" he doesn't mean that which is physical, but that which is fallen and sinful. Then he lists about a dozen sins that can be grouped into several categories: sinful uses of sex (v 5b) and money (v 5c), along with sinful attitudes (v 8a) and words (v 8b–9). Paul tells us that the wrath of God is coming on these sins (v 6). Though we once lived in them, we are now to put them all away (vv 7–8a). Paul is telling us to weed the sin out of the garden of our souls.

But notice what follows. In verses 9b–14, he tells us that having "put off," like an old set of clothes, "the old self with its practices," and having "put on the new self, which is being renewed in knowledge after the image of its creator" (v 10), we now must also "put on," like a new set of clothes, Christlike virtues such as compassion, kindness, humility, meekness, patience, forgiveness, and love (vv 12–14).

To put it simply, we must replace sins with graces. It's not enough to weed out the vices from the garden of the heart. We also have to cultivate the virtues, to grow the graces.

Spiritual disciplines in a spiritual community. "All this is well and good," you might say, "but how do I do that?" Verses 15–17 give a handful of practical answers, each relating to certain disciplines and practices that we must cultivate in our lives, and each answer given to the Christian community as a whole. This shows us that one of the most important ways to cultivate the graces of the Spirit is to practice spiritual disciplines in a spiritual community.

First is the practice of peacemaking. We must "let the peace of Christ" rule in our hearts (v 15). Christ came to bring peace into our relationships with one another, so we are to let his peace function as the umpire in our hearts. We are called together in one body, so our practices are to reflect that oneness.

But we also need to "let the word of Christ dwell in [us] richly, teaching and admonishing one another in all wisdom, singing psalms and hymns and spiritual songs" (v 16). This is the practice of rich, gospel-soaked, Scripture-saturated mutual ministry and worship.

Then verse 17 tells us to "do everything in the name of the Lord Jesus." This is the practice of worship fleshed out in everyday life, as we make honoring the name of Christ our conscious motive in all that we do.

Finally, there is the practice of gratitude, which is mentioned in each of these three verses: "Be thankful" (v 15). "[Sing] with thankfulness in your hearts to God" (v 16). "[Give] thanks to God the Father through him" (v 17).

The lesson is this: we can kill sin only when we cultivate the virtues of Christ and the graces of the Spirit in sin's place. And the only way to cultivate this kind of character is through the regular practices of Christian community: peacemaking, Scripture intake, admonishing one another, worship, and grateful prayer. These are the practices that help us set our affections on Christ and put our mouths out of taste for the deadly pleasures of sin by giving us greater satisfaction in him. [22]

Examine and Apply

1. Have you ever tried to deal with sin in legalistic ways? What was the result?

2. Have you ever experienced the "expulsive power of a new affection" that Thomas Chalmers described? Do you still experience it consistently?

3. When it comes to the Siren song of sin, are you more like Ulysses or Jason? What keeps you from seduction: the ropes of rules or the sound of a sweeter song in Jesus?

4. Are you giving due attention to cultivating the virtues of Christ in your life? Where do you need to balance "putting off" with "putting on"?

Seven

CRUCIFIED WITH CHRIST

How the Cross Kills Sin

The most graphic image that Scripture uses for the killing of sin is crucifixion. The cross has rightly stood at the center of Christian theology throughout church history. But the fact that we are so far removed culturally and temporally from the practice of crucifixion means that the potency of this image is easily lost on us.

You and I have never witnessed a crucifixion. Even the most violent and graphic depictions of crucifixions in films are cleaned-up versions of the most horrific and degrading form of torture and execution known in the ancient world.

Our generation has never seen a man crucified except in sugary religious art; but it was not a sweet sight, and few of us would dare to have a real picture of a crucifixion on our bedroom walls. A crucified slave beside the Roman road screamed until his voice died and then hung, a filthy, festering clot of flies, sometimes for days — a living man whose hands and feet were swollen masses of gangrenous meat. This is what our Lord took upon himself. [23]

Crucifixion was so painful that a word was invented to describe it: *excruciating*, which literally means "out of the cross." The Jewish historian Josephus said that to be crucified was to die a thousand deaths. The Roman historian Cicero said, "There is no fitting word that can possibly describe so horrible a deed" as crucifixion, and "the very word 'cross' should be far removed not only from the person of a Roman citizen, but from his thoughts, eyes, and his ears."[24]

With this background, we can begin to understand why it was so scandalous for Christians to serve a crucified King. But despite the scandal, Paul actually boasted in the cross and represented the life of a Christian as a crucified life, employing this graphic image as a metaphor for the believer's relationship with sin.

> For through the law I died to the law, so that I might live to God. I have been crucified with Christ. It is no longer I who live, but Christ who lives in me. And the life I now live in the flesh I live by faith in the Son of God, who loved me and gave himself for me. . . . And those who belong to Christ Jesus have crucified the flesh with its passions and desires. . . . But far be it from me to boast except in the cross of our Lord Jesus Christ, by which the world has been crucified to me, and I to the world. (Galatians 2:19–20, 5:24, 6:14)

What was it about crucifixion that led Paul to write this way, and what does it mean for us today?

The Cross and the Nature of Mortification

"Those who belong to Christ Jesus have crucified the flesh with its passions and desires," writes Paul in Galatians 5:24. These words depict the nature of a believer's break with sin in graphic but insightful terms. Sin's death is like a crucifixion: slow, gradual, painful, and eventually final.

The death sentence of sin. When a condemned criminal picked up his cross to carry it to the execution site, there was no turning back, no chance for reprieve, parole, or pardon. Crucifixion was a death sentence. But the death would be gradual, often taking not hours but days. When first nailed to the cross, the victim would struggle for survival, crying out in agony with all his might. But as he lost blood and strength, the struggle would lessen and his cries would grow faint.

Putting sin to death is a similar experience. There is a finality to the decisive break with sin to which our Lord calls us: "If anyone would come after me, let him deny himself and take up his cross and follow me" (Mark 8:34). Once we truly pick up our cross, having had our hearts changed by the grace of Christ to yield our lives to him, there is no turning back. The die has been cast, the future has been determined: sin must be killed. Taking up the cross to follow Jesus mean that sin has received a death sentence. But it doesn't die all at once. No, putting sin to death is a slow process.

Mortification is also a painful process, and we must never allow ourselves to think that the pain associated with sanctification is a sign that something is wrong. Crucifixion is painful, and Scripture presents mortification as a kind of crucifixion. The pain cannot be separated from the process.

At first, our sinful flesh struggles against the Spirit, screaming in agony to be spared. But mortification gradually weakens the power of sinful desires in our hearts. In the words of Octavius Winslow, "Nail after nail must pierce our corruptions, until the entire body of sin, each member thus transfixed, is crucified and slain."[25]

Leaving sin to die. Perhaps our biggest problem in dealing with sin is the half-heartedness of our commitment. Rather than making a decisive break with sin, we try to stop the big, bad, scandalous sins immediately, while weaning ourselves off the little sins in stages. We don't bear the fruit of holiness because the roots of repentance have not gone deep enough. As John R. W. Stott writes:

It is as if, having nailed our old nature to the cross, we keep wistfully returning to the scene of its execution. We begin to fondle it, to caress it, to long for its release, even to try to take it down again from the cross. We need to learn to leave it there. When some jealous, or proud, or malicious, or impure thought invades our mind we must kick it out at once. It is fatal to begin to examine it and consider whether we are going to give in to it or not. We have declared war on it; we are not going to resume negotiations. We have settled the issue for good; we are not going to re-open it. We have crucified the flesh; we are never going to draw the nails. [26]

The Cross and the Power of Mortification

The image of crucifixion provides a second and even more important insight about mortification. This truth is found in its connection to Christ's crucifixion for us. In Galatians 2, Paul points to our crucifixion with Christ: "I have been crucified with Christ," he writes. "It is no longer I who live, but Christ who lives in me. And the life I now live in the flesh I live by faith in the Son of God, who loved me and gave himself for me" (Galatians 2:20). It is significant that this *precedes* Paul's later statements in this letter about crucifying the flesh and being crucified to the world (Galatians 5:24, 6:14).

The death of sin in the death of Christ. This connection reminds us that the power of mortification comes directly from Christ crucified for us. As John Owen said, "The death of Christ is the death of sin."[27] Only by virtue of his death to sin as our representative do we receive the power to renounce sin in our lives.

This is also the teaching of Paul in Romans 6, where he says that "our old self was crucified with [Christ] ... so that we would no longer be enslaved to sin" (v 6). This is part of Paul's argument for why it is morally incongruous for a believer to continue to live in sin. Christ was crucified for sin (not his, but ours). In his death, "he died to sin, once for all" (v 10), meaning that he died to the judicial power and authority of sin. Since we died with him, sin has lost its power over us. "So," Paul says, "you also must consider yourselves dead to sin and alive to God in Christ Jesus. Let not sin therefore reign in your mortal body, to make you obey its passions" (vv 11–12).

This means that the *power* we need for crucifying sin comes from the cross, where Christ was crucified. It is only through virtue of *his* death to sin that you and I can put sin to death in *our* lives. The only way you can kill sin is through the power of the Spirit applying the death of Christ to your heart and life.

"Let us slay sin, for Christ was slain." Christ's effectual sin-canceling work of the cross is therefore the only power that will enable us to kill sin in our own lives. And this is one of the purposes for which he died. As Peter says, "He himself bore our sins in his body on the tree, that we might die to sin and live to righteousness. By his wounds you have been healed" (1 Peter 2:24).

As the great nineteenth-century preacher Charles Spurgeon, in one of his characteristically Christ-centered sermons, declared:

> The best preaching is, "We preach Christ crucified."
> The best living is, "We are crucified with Christ."
> The best man is a crucified man…The more we
> live beholding our Lord's unutterable griefs, and
> understanding how he has fully put away our sin,
> the more holiness shall we produce. The more we
> dwell where the cries of Calvary can be heard, where
> we can view heaven, and earth, and hell, all moved

by his wondrous passion—the more noble will our lives become. Nothing puts life into men like a dying Savior. Get you close to Christ, and carry the remembrance of him about you from day to day, and you will do right royal deeds. Come, let us slay sin, for Christ was slain. Come, let us bury all our pride, for Christ was buried. Come, let us rise to newness of life, for Christ has risen. [28]

The Cross and the Means of Mortification

We have been discussing the objective power of the cross of Christ to put our sins to death. This objective power is real and effectual, regardless of our feelings about it at any given point. But there is also a *subjective* element involved: we must *exercise faith in Christ and his cross* in order to enjoy the fruits of his victory over sin in our lives. As Paul goes on to say, "Far be it from me to boast except in the cross of our Lord Jesus Christ, by which the world has been crucified to me, and I to the world" (Galatians 6:14).

The cross not only shows us 1) the *nature* of mortification (a slow, gradual, painful death), and 2) the *power* of mortification (crucifixion with Christ). It also shows us 3) the *means* of mortification. In order to kill sin, we must exercise both faith and love. We exercise these graces by fixing our minds on and filling our affections with the cross of Christ.

Faith: fix your mind on the cross of Christ. When Paul describes his life as crucified with Christ, he says: "It is no longer I who live, but Christ who lives in me. And the life I now live in the flesh I live by *faith* in the Son of God, who loved me and gave himself for me" (Galatians 2:20). The crucified life is a life of *faith*.

As an illustration of the power of faith, consider the woman who had suffered a discharge of blood for twelve years. She experienced healing when she touched Jesus and power went out from him. Seeing her, Jesus said, "Daughter, your faith has made you well" (Mark 5:25–34). Faith is the hand that touches Christ, laying hold of his priestly robes to secure his healing power.

In his excellent book *The Enemy Within*, Kris Lundgaard reminds us that the greatest heroes and villains of stories and literature always have an Achilles' heel, some weakness that can lead to their ultimate undoing.

> Superman seems invincible. But if you can snake a pebble of Kryptonite into his boot, he'll crumble into a heap of blue and red.... The Wolfman will ravage the village every full moon — unless someone shoots him with a silver bullet. Count Dracula will drain Transylvania of its life — unless you can find him asleep in his coffin and pound a wooden stake through his heart. [29]

The Achilles' heel for sin is faith. "Faith is Kryptonite, a wooden stake, and a silver bullet all in one."[29a] If you want to kill sin, you must exercise faith.

Love: fill your affections with the cross of Christ. Faith must be joined with *love*, the two combined toward one purpose. Like water in a pipe, or electricity in a wire, they are not the same thing, but each is useless without the other. As Paul says in Galatians 5:6, we need "faith working through love."

Jesus, crucified and slain, is the great object of a believer's love. Our love answers his: "We love because he first loved us" (1 John 4:19). When we love him, we cling to him and become more like him. Just as an old husband and wife, deeply in love, cling tenaciously to one another and, in many ways, even begin to resemble one another, so love for Christ draws us to him and makes us like him.

How to do it. But how do we *practically* set our minds on and fill our affections with the cross? How do we exercise faith and love toward Christ crucified for us? It is not done with a crucifix or some other visual aid. This is not the method proposed in Scripture. No, Paul tells us how Christ is portrayed as crucified: "It was before your eyes [that is, through preaching] that Jesus Christ was publicly portrayed as crucified. Let me ask you only this: Did you receive the Spirit by works of the law or by hearing with faith?" (Galatians 3:1b–2).

The great object of our faith and love is Christ as portrayed in the gospel. Only as we gaze on the glory of the Lord in the gospel are we transformed by the Spirit (2 Corinthians 3:18). We do this as we:

1. Consider the purpose of Christ's death for us
2. With an expectation of help from him

Our Savior died to destroy the works of the Devil, to redeem us from lawlessness, and to cleanse and sanctify us through his blood.

- When you meditate on the mercy and compassion of Christ, the mighty Maker who died in your place.
- When you remember that your ransom was purchased at the price of his precious blood.
- When you consider the cost of the gifts you have received through the cross — wisdom, righteousness, holiness, sonship, redemption, and future resurrection to glory forever.
- When you reflect on the salvation and safety that your Brother, your Captain, and your King has secured for you.
- When you realize that God is more satisfied with Jesus' obedience than he was grieved by your sins.
- When you ponder the pain and the shame of the scourging and scoffing, the spitting and mocking, the crown of thorns and the nails in his hands, and all the cruel wounds he received on your behalf.
- When you understand that you are not only acquitted but accepted as fully righteous in God's sight, *perfect* in the eyes of the law, because the full measure of divine wrath was poured out on Jesus for you, and his obedience has been counted as yours.
- When your heart is filled with the glories of his triumph over Satan, sin, and death.
- When your affections are captured anew by the self-sacrificing love of the Lord and Lover of your soul…

…*then* you will discover that the stranglehold of sin on your heart has grown weaker, that sin is less alluring, and that your fallen desires have been displaced by desires for God, his glory, and his grace.

My sin, oh, the bliss of this glorious thought!
My sin, not in part but the whole,
Is nailed to the cross, and I bear it no more,
Praise the Lord, praise the Lord, O my soul! [30]

When you are fighting sin, fill your mind with these truths. Say: "Lord Jesus, you died to free me from sin, to put my sinful passions and desires to death, to change me and restore me in your glorious image. Thank you for your dying love! Now, cleanse me with your blood. Strengthen me with your power. Uphold me by your grace. Help me, Lord!" This posture of dependent faith and zealous love toward the Savior who was slain for us is lethal to sin.

Examine and Apply

1. Have you made a decisive break with sin? Or, having nailed sin to the cross, are you guilty of trying to nurse it back to health?

2. Do you live with regular consciousness of your union with Christ? Paul tells us to consider ourselves dead to sin and alive to God in Christ Jesus, and *on that basis* to not let sin reign in our mortal bodies. Is this how you personally fight sin?

3. Have you experienced the sin-killing power of the cross of Christ? Next time you are faced with a temptation to sin (or a sinful desire or action to mortify), fill your mind and heart with the cross of Christ. Having read this chapter, put in your own words how you would go about doing this.

Eight
EMPOWERED BY THE SPIRIT

His Role and Ours

Have you ever been confused about the role of the Holy Spirit in living the Christian life? I have.

The Holy Spirit is a favorite teaching topic for youth camps, evangelistic crusades, and missions conferences. Sometimes the speaker is calm and serene, exuding the appearance of ineffable and elusive (and supernatural) peace of mind. Sometimes he is loud and sweaty, with what appears to be inexhaustible energy (which comes, of course, from the Holy Spirit). Both types invite you to give up the "self-life" for the "Christ-life," to stop "striving in the energy of the flesh" and start "living in the power of the Spirit," to "quit trying and start trusting." Sometimes they say that you already have the Spirit, but you are not surrendered enough. "You don't need more of the Spirit. He just needs to have more of you!" Sometimes they hold out hope for more of the Spirit: a second "baptism" or a fresh "filling."

You want whatever it is that you don't have, but your mind is more than a bit muddled about exactly what that is. You get the impression that to step into this inviting Spirit-filled life requires something of you, but you're not sure what. Usually words such as *surrender* and *yielding* pop up. On one hand, you feel convicted. "Yes, of course, I need to be more yielded to God. Spirit of the living God, fall fresh on me." On the other hand, you feel discouraged. You want to yield yourself to the Lord, to fully surrender and obey. But if this is the condition for walking in the power of the Spirit, you're not sure you'll ever qualify. "I've done this before. I guess I'm still not surrendered enough." If you need to obey in order to get grace, where will you find the grace to obey? You are told that surrender is simply "an act of the will." But your will seems to be that which gives you the most trouble!

If you experience this long enough, you may start to feel bipolar, as if you are riding an emotional see-saw. Sometimes you exude joyful hope that you've finally discovered the Spirit-filled life, and at other times you feel down, discouraged, and depressed, wondering if you are even saved.

The root of your confusion is that you don't know what the Spirit actually does and what you're expected to do. You can't tell the difference between living "in your own strength" and living "in the strength of the Spirit."

I understand this confusion and felt it often in the early years of my formation and growth as a Christian. I'm sure there were many reasons why I was so confused, but one of the main reasons was that the relationship between the Spirit's role and my role wasn't clear. Exhortations to "stop trying and start trusting" were confusing and, I would argue, even misleading, because they left the impression that all of my effort and struggle against sin reflected trust in the flesh rather than the Spirit. A sharp and unbiblical division was placed between the Spirit's power and my effort, leaving the impression that if I was struggling against sin in any way, I must not be relying on the Spirit.

But the Scriptures give us a more balanced perspective. On one hand, the Bible *does* exhort us to "walk by" and be "filled with" the Spirit, and to not "grieve" or "quench" the Spirit (Galatians 5:25; Ephesians 5:18, 4:30; 1 Thessalonians 5:19). Over and over again, the Christian life is described in terms of the Spirit's work in and through us. But on the other hand, Scripture never speaks of the Spirit's work in ways that eviscerate our responsibility to actively pursue holiness. We are called not only to *walk* in the Spirit but also to *run* the race set before us, to *flee* from sin, to *pursue* godly virtues, and to *fight* the good fight of faith (Hebrews 12:1, 1 Timothy 6:11–12).

Did you notice the words in italics? The Bible uses lots of active verbs when it talks about living the Christian life. Scripture does not present the work of the Spirit as that which relieves us of the need for effort but as that which empowers our effort. "Souls that cultivate passivity do not thrive, but waste away," writes J. I. Packer, "The Christian's motto should not be 'Let go and let God' but 'Trust God and get going!'"[31]

Nowhere is this more necessary than in how we deal with sin, for Scripture makes it clear that the responsibility for killing sin is ours. Yet Paul also says that we must put sin to death "by the Spirit" (Romans 8:13). So, the Spirit has a role and so do we. In this chapter, we're going to consider both: the Spirit's role in supplying grace in the pursuit of holiness and our role in cooperating with his work.

The Spirit's Role: Supplying Us with Grace

Jesus promised to send his disciples God the Holy Spirit, the third person of the Trinity, and he kept that promise on the day of Pentecost, when he poured his Spirit out on the church. This was a significant event, as unique in salvation history as Jesus' crucifixion, resurrection, and exaltation. Ever since that day, the Spirit has continued to abide in the church, supplying God's people with grace, leading them into the fullness of Christ.

The Spirit works in several ways to supply grace for killing our sins.

The Spirit purifies and cleanses our hearts. The prophets often linked the work of the Spirit to images of fire and water—fire that purifies and water that cleanses. John the Baptist combined these images when he said that the Messiah would come baptizing with the Holy Spirit and with fire (Matthew 3:11). Jesus spoke of spiritual cleansing when he told Nicodemus that unless one is born of water and the Spirit, one cannot enter the kingdom of God (John 3:5). The Spirit burns away the root of sin in our hearts and makes us clean. This process begins, of course, in the new birth, but it continues throughout our earthly lives. But the Spirit's work doesn't end there.

The Spirit opens our minds to the fullness of Christ as revealed in the gospel. He takes the medicine of the gospel and applies it to our wounded hearts. He gives us communion with Christ in his sufferings and death. This is why Jesus called him "the Spirit of truth" and said that he would bear witness to Christ (John 15:26).

<u>The Spirit causes our hearts to abound in grace.</u> He produces his fruit in our lives (Galatians 5:19–21). By doing his work of grace in our hearts, the Spirit develops the character of Christ within us, conforming us to his divine image. This positive spiritual growth works directly against the presence of sin in us. As the Spirit renews and restores us, the graces of love, joy, peace, patience, kindness, goodness, faithfulness, gentleness, and self-control develop, grow, and flourish. These graces are directly contrary to the thriving of indwelling sin.

Our Role:
Cooperating with the Spirit

So what is our role in living the Christian life? It's important to emphasize that Scripture repeatedly makes the *duty* of mortification *ours*. Though we cannot do this apart from the Spirit, neither does the Spirit work in such a way as to subvert our responsibility. As John Owen rightly said, the Spirit "works in us and with us, not against us or without us."[32] The question, then, is how do we cooperate with his work?

<u>Remembering that the Spirit supplies the grace of Christ to our souls, we need to actively seek him for grace.</u> To paraphrase G. Campbell Morgan, we know that we cannot *control* the Spirit any more than can we can control the wind. But like a sailor at sea, we can "set

good

our sails" to catch the Spirit's wind when he blows. God has given us various ways of setting the sails, but the most essential ones are prayer and meditation on Scripture. We will consider these in more detail in the next chapter.

We must nurture the fruit of the Spirit in our lives. As noted above, the Spirit produces fruit in us. But we must be cultivating all dimensions of the character of Christ, giving special attention to the virtues that most directly counter the specific sins to which we are prone. For example, if you have a disposition toward lustful thoughts, you need to cultivate self-control in your thought life. If you have a tendency to become anxious and worried, develop the virtue of peace in all circumstances. If you are easily angered, nurture the grace of patience. With the Spirit's help, search out your unique inclinations toward sin. Then ask the Lord to help you develop the opposite virtues in their place.

We must respond with repentance when the Spirit convicts us of sin. If we habitually open our hearts to his searching gaze, he will come like fire to burn away the impurities of our hearts and like water to cleanse us from the filth of our sins.

There is a wonderful scene in *The Pilgrim's Progress* in which Christian, in his journey from the City of Destruction to the Celestial City, learns an important lesson in the Interpreter's House. Christian sees a "fire burning against a wall, and one standing by it always, casting much water upon it to quench it. Yet did the fire burn higher and hotter." He asks the Interpreter what this means and is told that "the fire is the work of grace that is wrought in the heart; he that casts water upon it to extinguish and put it out is the Devil." Then the Interpreter takes him to the back side of the wall to show him why the fire burns higher and hotter rather than going out. To his astonishment, Christian sees a man who is continually, though secretly, casting oil onto the fire. The Interpreter tells him that "this is Christ, who continually, with the oil of his grace maintains the work already begun in the heart, by means of which, notwithstanding what the Devil can do, the souls of his people prove gracious still."[33] This is an encouraging picture of how Christ, through his Spirit, supplies the "oil" of his grace to empower and sustain the work of sanctification and mortification in the hearts of his people.

Examine and Apply

1. Have you been too passive in your approach to sanctification? Has this chapter helped clarify the relationship between the Spirit's work and your effort in pursuing holiness?

2. How have you experienced the work of the Spirit in your heart in the past week? Is he convicting you of sin? Urging you toward obedience? Opening your mind and heart to the beauty of Christ and the gospel?

3. How can you more consciously depend on the Spirit in your daily life? What are some practical things you can do to "set the sails" so as to catch the Spirit's wind?

Nine
THE WEAPONS OF WAR

Meditation and Prayer

A great general once said, "In time of war it is the worst mistake to underrate your enemy, and try to make a little war!"[34] Too many of us underrate the power and malignancy of indwelling sin and try to make a little war. We don't see sin the way God sees sin. If we did, we would find it repulsive and repugnant, and we would fight it with all our strength.

This book is about mortification, the Christian duty of killing sin. We have learned what mortification actually is and why it is necessary. We have taken an inside look at indwelling sin and have analyzed the pattern of temptation. And we have seen that the only way to put sin to death is through the transforming power of the gospel as we fill our minds and hearts with the cross of Christ and cooperate with the work of the Spirit.

While I have woven the threads of application into the fabric of these chapters, the question of how practically to mortify sin deserves more precise explanation.

So in this final chapter, I want to look at a crucial set of disciplines that God has given us for killing sin: meditation and prayer. These are our most effective weapons in the war against sin. As the Psalmist wrote, "How can a young man keep his way pure? By guarding it according to your word. With my whole heart I seek you; let me not wander from your commandments! I have stored up your word in my heart, that I might not sin against you" (Psalms 119:9–11).

Without These, You Will Not Grow

For centuries, believers have maintained that God's Word and prayer are indispensable to progressive sanctification. John Owen, for example, said that prayer and meditation on Scripture are duties "which are especially apt to weaken and subdue the whole law of sin at its heart and ... believers should give particular attention to these all their lives. They are health-restoring remedies against the disease of sin."[35] This is standard advice in the classic Puritan manuals on holiness, and for good reason: Scripture itself teaches us to meditate and pray for the sake of sanctification. "How can a young man keep his way pure?" asks the psalmist. Answer: "By guarding it according to your word" (Psalms 119:9). But how do we guard our way with the Word? The twofold answer is *prayer* ("With my whole heart I seek you; let me not wander from your commandments!" [v 10]) and *meditation* ("I have stored up your word in my heart, that I might not sin against you" [v 11]).

In John 15, Jesus teaches us that he is the vine and we are the branches, and that apart from him we can do nothing. It is only through abiding in him that we bear fruit. But what does abiding in Jesus look like? He answers: "If you abide in me, and *my words abide in you*, ask whatever you wish, and it will be done for you" (v 7). We abide in Jesus when his words abide in us. And when Paul describes the believer's warfare against spiritual forces of evil, he exhorts us to put on the whole armor of God (Ephesians 6:10–18), including "the sword of the Spirit, which is the *word of God, praying* at all times in the Spirit, with all prayer and supplication" (vv 17–18).

But despite this testimony of Scripture, it is possible that you feel disappointed, even disillusioned, when you hear yet another pastor tell you that what's missing in your battle against sin is more Bible reading and prayer. For many people, this counsel has worn thin. They have tried to have consistent quiet times, but they find the discipline not only difficult to maintain but of little spiritual benefit. The last thing they want to hear is, "Read your Bible and pray." Such advice might even smack of legalism.

I am sensitive to this reaction because I relate to the struggle. I have gone through seasons when I found it very difficult to maintain spiritual disciplines. I know what it is like to crack open my Bible in the hope of feeding my soul with rich food, only to feel like I'm eating dry cereal. Sometimes I feel as if my prayers never get through the rafters of my house.

But I have also experienced the transforming power of God's Spirit working through these means of grace. I have seen the sin-killing power of the Word of God and have walked in the freedom of the Spirit in response to prayer. The truth is that we sell ourselves short in the spiritual disciplines. Like lifelong dieters who are always looking for a magic pill instead of developing a long-term lifestyle of exercise and nutrition, we approach spiritual disciplines wrongly, expecting overnight results and quitting when our quiet times don't deliver. As G. K. Chesterton once said: "The Christian ideal has not been tried and found wanting. It has been found difficult; and left untried."[36]

So, when your experience doesn't line up with the testimony of other believers and *especially* with that of Scripture, don't be too quick to write off that testimony as unhelpful. You need to bring your heart and practice into alignment with the wisdom of the Word. The Word *does* sanctify: "Christ loved the church and gave himself up for her, that he might sanctify her, having cleansed her by the washing of water with the word" (Ephesians 5:25b–26). "Sanctify them in the truth; your word is truth" (John 17:17). And we *should* pray for holiness with the confident expectation that our faithful God will make us holy: "May the Lord make you increase and abound in love for one another and for all, as we do for you, so that he may establish your hearts blameless in holiness before our God and Father, at the coming of our Lord Jesus with all his saints" (1 Thessalonians 3:12–13). If you are disillusioned with the disciplines of meditation and prayer, the problem isn't that this remedy does not work, but that you haven't applied it with the appropriate intention and necessary intensity.

Remember, while we are absolutely dependent on God's grace to empower us, his grace makes us active, not passive. Yes, through Christ God has done what we could never do for ourselves. He has redeemed us from the curse of the law, and rescued us from the power of sin and death. But he also equips us with his Word, invites us to prayer, and enables us by his Spirit to actually do what we must do in order to make genuine progress.

How Meditation and Prayer Mortify Sin

The disciplines of meditation and prayer are intended for holiness, which includes both the mortification of sin and the cultivation of godly character. How do these disciplines work to mortify sin?

Meditation and prayer aid self-examination. God's Word is a sharp, double-edged scalpel that lays bare the thoughts and motives of our hearts (Hebrews 4:12). In prayer, we come into the presence of our God, in whose sight we are fully known and exposed (Hebrews 4:13). When we open the Scriptures, the living God speaks to us; when we pray, we speak to him. If we approach these disciplines not simply as duties to be performed but as the means of knowing God, they will cause us to examine ourselves.

When we meditate and pray, we should consider our lives, asking the Lord to know our hearts, test our thoughts, and search out any wicked ways within us (Psalms 139:23–24). In this humble posture, we ask the Spirit to bring to light all the covert operations of sin in our hearts.

"In real prayer," writes Owen,

> the Spirit of God gives his assistance, even in discover-
> ing the secret workings of the law of sin. ... The Spirit
> gives a holy, spiritual light to the mind, enabling it
> to search the dark recesses of the heart and find the
> subtle and deceitful schemes of the law of sin. These
> are apprehended, brought into the presence of God,
> judged, condemned, and lamented. What can possibly
> be more effectual for their ruin and destruction? [37]

**Meditation and prayer expose the sinful thoughts
and desires that hold our hearts.** Meditation and prayer
are duties of such a spiritual nature that the flesh finds
them distasteful. We can be sure that if there are any sinful
desires lying covert in our souls, they will rise in violent
opposition against us when we set ourselves to seek God.
The flesh will do everything in its power to survive the
lethal wounds of God's holy Word. Evil thoughts will
intrude, sinful passions will distract, and self-justifying
rationalizations will kick in. When this happens, the very
sins that we need to kill are showing themselves.

**Meditation and prayer deepen our sense of sin's
vileness and renew our hatred of it.** As we saw in
chapter four, sin is deceptive and does its tempting work
by confusing the mind and enticing the affections. When
the mind is taken off its guard, sin begins to look satisfying. Our hearts are hardened by the deceitfulness of sin
(Hebrews 3:13). But as we meditate on God's Word and
pray, we submit both our minds and affections to the

Holy Spirit. The masks of sin are removed and we see it again in its true colors. As we regain a sense of the vileness of sin, our hatred of it is renewed and our souls are freshly engaged to oppose it in all its forms.

Meditation and prayer strengthen our faith in the sin-killing power of the cross. The only power that is effective for killing sin is the grace of Christ, purchased on the cross and applied to our hearts by the Holy Spirit. But this power is mediated to us through faith, and faith is nourished and strengthened through the Word and prayer.

How to Use These Weapons Effectively

Finally, let's consider the most effective ways to wield these weapons:

Remember that meditation and prayer are means for communion with God. The goal of spiritual disciplines is to draw near to God. One of the reasons our "devotional" lives fail is that we neglect the *devotional* element. We focus on accumulating information instead of fostering friendship with God. We forget that the disciplines are means of grace in which the Lord himself strengthens us. When we meditate and pray, we're not spending time by ourselves but with God himself! We can see this in Psalm 119, where almost every one of the 176 verses both addresses the Lord in prayer and reflects on some aspect of his self-revelation in Scripture. As we read the psalm, we quickly realize that the psalmist is talking *to* God *about* his Word. This is what Owen meant when he said that we should "meditate *of* God *with* God."[38]

When we meditate, we're not simply pondering propositions. We are setting our minds on God himself in his glories, attributes, works, and ways. This means that we must never approach Scripture as detached observers of a text. When we come to God's Word, we not only read it, it reads us. When we pray, we speak not to the wall but to the Lover of our souls, the One who purchased our pardon at the price of his own blood. These devotional disciplines are not self-help techniques. They are pathways to fellowship with the triune God himself.

Meditate and pray with your eyes peeled for Jesus. Remember to keep Jesus himself central in the Word and prayer. Sometimes believers leave the gospel behind in their practice of the disciplines. Prayer is seen as duty more than privilege. Meditation, if engaged in at all, is more about amassing interesting bits of Bible trivia than deepening our delight in the Savior. Maybe we've missed something.

Think about the prayers in the New Testament. Read Paul's prayers in his letters and, every time you find a reference to Jesus, circle it. You will be stunned by the pervasive centrality of Christ. Though Christians often end their prayers in Jesus' name, we tend to take the privilege of prayer for granted. We need to remember that our only access to God in prayer is through Jesus Christ. That's why we pray in his name. He is the High Priest who gives us boldness to come before the throne of grace (Hebrews 4:15–16). "For through *him* we ... have access in one Spirit to the Father" (Ephesians 2:18). We need to be Christ-centered in our prayers.

The same is true for our practice of meditating on Scripture. In John 5, Jesus rebuked the most astute biblical scholars of his day for missing him in their study of the Old Testament Scriptures: "You search the Scriptures because you think that in them you have eternal life; and it is they that bear witness about me, yet you refuse to come to me that you may have life" (vv 39–40). It is possible to know a lot about the Bible and still miss the main point.

Walking with two of his disciples on the road to Emmaus, Jesus began with Moses and all the prophets and "interpreted to them in all the Scriptures the things concerning himself" (Luke 24:27). When the disciples later reflected on their experience, they said, "Did not our hearts burn within us while he talked to us on the road, while he opened to us the Scriptures?" (v 32). One of the reasons some people fail to benefit from their study of Scripture is that they interpret it in gospel-ignoring, Christ-neglecting ways. If your Bible study is nothing more than churning out of the historical narratives of Scripture a series of pious platitudes, "life lessons," and moral maxims, do not wonder if your heart isn't radically changed. Good advice doesn't produce burning hearts.

We need to learn to read the Scriptures as Isaac Watts did. In one of his hymns, Watts said:

> Laden with guilt, and full of fears,
> I fly to Thee, my Lord,
> And not a glimpse of hope appears
> But in Thy written Word.
> The volume of my Father's grace

> Does all my griefs assuage;
> Here I behold my Savior's face
> In every page. [39]

The only way we will be deeply changed by our meditation on Scripture is to behold our Savior's face on every page. This means learning to read the Old Testament in light of the New and to see the many stories of Scripture in their relation to the meta-narrative of creation, fall, redemption, and new creation. It means tracing the various themes of Scripture (such as covenant and kingdom; law and grace; temple and sacrifice; word and wisdom; prophet, priest, and king; and more) to their ultimate fulfillment in Jesus. Only by developing a Christ-centered instinct in reading Scripture will we behold his glory. [40] Only then will we be changed: "And we all, with unveiled face, beholding the glory of the Lord, are being transformed into the same image from one degree of glory to another. For this comes from the Lord who is the Spirit" (2 Corinthians 3:18).

Meditate and pray with others. Don't ignore community. One of the most neglected sources of grace in our self-sufficient, individualistic culture is the church. In his short but stout letter to the saints, Jude says, "But you, beloved, building yourselves up in your most holy faith and praying in the Holy Spirit, keep yourselves in the love of God, waiting for the mercy of our Lord Jesus Christ that leads to eternal life" (Jude 20–21). There are two things to notice in those verses. First, Jude is writing to a group of believers, not an individual. Second, he tells them that the way to keep themselves in the love of God is to build themselves up in the faith and pray in the Holy Spirit. The Word and prayer—with others.

Sometimes we forget that most of Paul's letters were written to churches. When he exhorts us to kill our sins and grow in grace, he speaks in a corporate context. We pursue holiness *together*. There are several aspects to this. There is, first of all, the public ministry of the Word and prayer. Paul tells Timothy to preach the Word, both in season and out of season, because it is "breathed out by God and profitable for teaching, for reproof, for correction, and for training in righteousness" (2 Timothy 3:16). The apostles of Jerusalem gave themselves "to prayer and to the ministry of the word" (Acts 6:4), believing that this was one of the most important ways they could serve other believers.

But we also need the private, and more personal, ministry of mutual admonition and exhortation. This is why Hebrews says: "Take care, brothers, lest there be in any of you an evil, unbelieving heart, leading you to fall away from the living God. But exhort one another every day, as long as it is called 'today,' that none of you may be hardened by the deceitfulness of sin" (3:12–13). We need one another.

Finally, we should not neglect the broader communion of saints throughout history. The Lord has given us rich resources for spiritual growth in many of the books written by believers of the past. I learned most of the insights I have shared in this book from Owen, the seventeenth-century Puritan pastor and theologian. Do yourself a favor and read some old books! Your walk with Christ will be enriched.

Examine and Apply

1. What is the quality of your devotional life? (Circle one)

    a. Nonexistent

    b. Sporadic and unsatisfying

    c. Dry cereal—more duty than delight

    d. Consistently nourishing

2. When you attempt to meditate or pray, what kinds of thoughts, feelings, and desires flood into your mind? Self-satisfaction? Discouragement? Anxiety? Lust? Guilt? How might these intrusions be an indication of the very sins you need to put to death?

3. Do you think much about Jesus when you meditate and pray?

Appendix 1
Does Romans 7:14–25 Describe a Believer?

Chapter 3 is written with the assumption that, in Romans 7:14–25, Paul is describing a believer's experience of ongoing conflict with indwelling sin. But not all interpreters agree, so it is worth asking about the spiritual condition of the speaker in the passage. Is it Paul speaking about himself as a believer, as an unbeliever, or as something in between? Or is he speaking not of himself but of someone else? This book, of course, is not the context for rehearsing the whole debate—see the commentaries on Romans for that. But here are several reasons why I believe Paul is describing his own experience as a believer with indwelling sin:

Paul writes in the present tense. This is an abrupt change from the previous verses (vv 7–13), where Paul describes his past experience with the law of God. Having shown how God's good and holy law has revealed the exceeding sinfulness of sin, he switches to the present tense and says, "For we know that the law is spiritual, but *I am of the flesh, sold under sin*" (v 14). What follows is a description of the inner turmoil he experiences as he finds himself acting contrary to his desires to do good. The present tense is sustained throughout.

Paul expresses his approval of and delight in God's law. In verses 14 and 16, he affirms that the law is spiritual and good. Then, in verse 22, he expresses his delight in God's law in his inner being, while in verse 25 he says that he serves the law of God with his mind. These do not seem to be the kinds of statements an unregenerate person would make. Paul says elsewhere that "the natural person does not accept the things of the Spirit of God, for they are folly to him, and he is not able to understand them because they are spiritually discerned" (1 Corinthians 2:14) and that the mind set on the flesh "does not submit to God's law; indeed, it cannot" (Romans 8:7). Furthermore, Paul uses the phrase "inner being" (v 22) or "inner self" only two other times (2 Corinthians 4:16, Ephesians 3:16), each referring to the inner nature of a Christian.

Paul expresses antagonism against sin. Paul also clearly hates the evil that he does (v 15) and recognizes the utter corruption of his sinful disposition (vv 17–18, 21). Then he expresses his mortal conflict with sin and the misery this brings into his life: "I see in my members another law waging war against the law of my mind and making me captive to the law of sin that dwells in my members. Wretched man that I am! Who will deliver me from this body of death?" (vv 23–24). This is a very different picture from what we get in Philippians 3, where Paul describes his condition before Christ as a confident, legalistic, and self-righteous Pharisee.

Paul expresses Christian hope. We see Paul's hope in verse 25, which ends with a summarizing statement of the inner conflict he has been describing: "Thanks be to God through Jesus Christ our Lord! So then, I myself serve the law of God with my mind, but with my flesh I serve the law of sin."

This interpretation harmonizes with Paul's theology elsewhere (for example, Galatians 5:16–17). Though many competent scholars disagree with this position, these observations have persuaded me that Paul wrote these words as a believer who was well acquainted with the ongoing conflict against indwelling sin, and that this passage therefore speaks directly to us in our own struggles against sin.

Appendix 2
For Further Reading

Fighting sin is a lifelong battle for which we need much help. I hope that this book will serve as a primer for many who will want to dig deeper into the doctrines of mortification and sanctification. Here are some resources to consider for further reading. I have divided them into three reading levels: basic, intermediate, and advanced.

Basic

Jerry Bridges, *The Discipline of Grace: God's Role and Our Role in the Pursuit of Holiness* (NavPress, 2006)

Kris Lundgaard, *The Enemy Within: Straight Talk about the Power and Defeat of Sin* (P & R, 1998)

John Owen, *The Mortification of Sin: Abridged and Made Easy to Read by Richard Rushing* (Banner of Truth Trust, 2004)

John Owen, *Indwelling Sin in Believers* (Banner of Truth Trust, 2010)

John Owen, *Temptation: Resisted and Repulsed* (Banner of Truth Trust, 2007)

John Owen, *The Holy Spirit: Abridged and Made Easy to Read by R. J. K. Law* (Banner of Truth Trust, 1998)

Intermediate

Brian G. Hedges, *Christ Formed in You: The Power of the Gospel for Personal Change* (Shepherd Press, 2010)

John Owen, *Overcoming Sin and Temptation*, Justin Taylor and Kelly Kapic, eds. (Crossway, 2006)

J. I. Packer, *Keep in Step with the Spirit: Finding Fullness in Our Walk with God* (Baker, 2005)

J. I. Packer, "The Spirituality of John Owen," in *A Quest for Godliness: The Puritan Vision of the Christian Life* (Crossway, 2010)

John Piper, *Future Grace* (Multnomah, 2005)

John Piper, *When I Don't Desire God: How to Fight for Joy* (Crossway, 2004)

J. C. Ryle, *Holiness: Its Nature, Hindrances, Difficulties, and Roots* (Charles Nolan, 2001)

Advanced

Sinclair Ferguson, *John Owen on the Christian Life* (Banner of Truth Trust, 1987)

Randall C. Gleason, *John Calvin and John Owen on Mortification: A Comparative Study in Reformed Spirituality* (Peter Lang, 1995)

John Owen, *The Works of John Owen, volumes 3, 6, and 7* (Banner of Truth Trust, 1966)

David Peterson, *Possessed by God: A New Testament Theology of Sanctification and Holiness* (Intervarsity, 2001)

Endnotes

1. John Owen, *The Mortification of Sin: Abridged and Made Easy to Read by Richard Rushing* (Banner ofTruthTrust, 2004), 5
2. C. S. Lewis, *Mere Christianity* (HarperOne, 1952, 1980), 92
3. These are fictional examples, not anecdotes about actual people I know.
4. Owen, 41
5. Ralston chronicled his life-or-death drama in his 2004 autobiography, *Between a Rock and a Hard Place*. His story was also told in the 2010 film, *127 Hours*.
6. C. S. Lewis, *The Pilgrim's Regress* (Eerdmans, 1943), 188–189
7. Thomas Vincent, quoted in John Blanchard, *Whatever Happened to Hell?* (Crossway, 1995), 145
8. Owen, 85
9. Robert Robertson, "ComeThou Fount of Every Blessing," 1758
10. This poem has been attributed to both John Bunyan (1628-1688) and John Berridge (1716-1793).Though often cited in books and sermons, I have been unable to locate the original source.
11. Dietrich Bonhoeffer, *Creation and Fall &Temptation:Two Biblical Studies* (Touchstone, 1997), 132
12. As told by J. I. Packer in *A Quest for Godliness:The Puritan Vision of the Christian Life* (Crossway Books, 2010 reprint), 194
13. Owen, 66
14. John Calvin, JohnT. McNeil, ed., Ford L. Battles, trans., *Institutes of the Christian Religion*, 1.1.2 (Westminster Press, 1960), 37
15. Kris Lundgaard, *The EnemyWithin: StraightTalk about the Power and Defeat of Sin* (P & R Publishing, 1998), 128
16. John Owen, *The Works of John Owen*, Vol. 2, 165. Emphasis added.
17. JeremyTaylor, quoted in *ChristianityToday,* March 2008, Vol. 52, No. 3
18. CharlesWesley, "Christ the Lord Is RisenToday," 1739
19. Thomas Chalmers, "The Expulsive Power of a New Affection," in AndrewWatterson Blackwood, comp., *The Protestant Pulpit: An Anthology of Master Sermons from the Reformation to Our Own Day* (Abingdon, 1947), 50, 56

20. I first heard this application of the stories of Ulysses, Jason, and the Sirens from Sam Storms.

21. Matthew Henry, quoted in John Piper, *Desiring God: The Meditations of a Christian Hedonist* (Multnomah, 2003), 12

22. For more on how a superior satisfaction in Jesus triumphs over the pleasures of sin, see John Piper's books *Future Grace* (Multnomah, 2005), and *Battling Unbelief: Defeating Sin with Superior Pleasure* (Multnomah, 2007).

23. Joy Davidman, *Smoke on the Mountain* (Westminster Press, 1954), 20

24. Cicero, quoted in Gordon D. Fee, *Paul's Letter to the Philippians* (Eerdmans, 1995), 217–218

25. Octavius Winslow, *No Condemnation in Christ Jesus* (The Banner of Truth Trust, 1991), 151

26. John R. W. Stott, *The Message of Galatians* (InterVarsity, 1984), 151–152

27. John Owen, *The Holy Spirit: Abridged and Made Easy to Read by R. J. K. Law* (The Banner of Truth Trust, 1998), 175

28. C. H. Spurgeon, "To Lovers of Jesus – An Example" in The Metropolitan Tabernacle Pulpit (Pilgrim Publications, 1977 reprint) Sermon #1834. This sermon is also available online at: http://www.spurgeongems.org/vols31-33/chs1834.pdf. Accessed June 12, 2011.

29. Lundgaard, 141

29a. Ibid., 142

30. Horatio Spafford, "It Is Well with My Soul," 1873

31. J. I. Packer, *Keep in Step with the Spirit: Finding Fullness in Our Walk with God* (Baker, 2005), 128

32. Owen, *Mortification of Sin*, 19

33. John Bunyan, *The Pilgrim's Progress* (New York: New American Library, 1981), 37

34. Quoted in J. C. Ryle, *Holiness: Its Nature, Hindrances, Difficulties, and Roots* (Epworth, England: Evangelical Press, reprint), 53

35. John Owen, *Indwelling Sin in Believers* (Banner of Truth Trust, 2010), 71

36. G. K. Chesterton, *What's Wrong with the World* (Adamant Media, 2005 reprint), 43

37. Owen, *Indwelling Sin*, 73

38. Ibid., 72, emphasis added

39. Isaac Watts, "Laden with Guilt and Full of Fears," 1709

40. Abundant helps are available for the eager student of Scripture. For starters, I would recommend the sermons of Tim Keller, senior pastor of Redeemer Presbyterian Church in New York City (http://www.redeemer.com/) and the following books:

Christopher J. H. Wright, *Knowing Jesus Through the Old Testament* (InterVarsity, 1992)

Vaughan Roberts, *God's Big Picture: Tracing the Storyline of the Bible* (InterVarsity, 2002)

Graeme Goldsworthy, *The Goldsworthy Trilogy: Gospel and Kingdom, Gospel and Wisdom, The Gospel in Revelation* (Paternoster, 2001)

Mark Dever, *The Message of the Old Testament: Promises Made* (Crossway, 2006)

Acknowledgments

I owe a great debt to the seventeenth-century Congregationalist pastor and theologian John Owen. His treatises on indwelling sin, temptation, the mortification of sin, and the Holy Spirit have not only provided deep nourishment to my soul, but formed the subtext of this book. I have been selective with quotes, but the substance of Owen's thought, the structure of his arguments, and even some of his phrases run through this book like rebar through concrete. To trace all the links, you'll have to read Owen for yourself.

I am also very grateful for J. I. Packer, Sinclair Ferguson, and Kris Lundgaard, whose books inspired me to dig deeper and read Owen for myself. Packer's *Quest for Godliness* sent me on a trek through the Puritans. They are redwoods indeed. Ferguson's *John Owen on the Christian Life* has been immensely helpful, both in unpacking Owen's theology and in feeding my soul with rich food. Lundgaard's *The Enemy Within* is an excellent model of bringing Owen's theology into the 21st century. It is also one of the most heart-searching books I've read and one of very few books to which I keep returning.

Thanks to Kevin Meath for the invitation to write for Cruciform Press. Kevin did a superb job editing my first book, and I was confident that the combination of his sharp editorial skills and his vibrant love for Christ and the church would make my second book a better one.

Closer to home, I'm grateful for my father, Ronnie Hedges, on whose shelves I saw *The Works of John Owen* all through my growing-up years. (Those thick, green books were so intimidating and uninteresting back then!) If Dad hadn't read the Puritans, I probably wouldn't have read them either. More importantly, he has provided a consistent example of holiness for as long as I can remember.

I want to express my deepest love and appreciation to my beautiful wife, Holly, and our three precious children, Stephen, Matthew, and Susannah. They bear with me and my sins more than anyone else. And they are the most frequent instruments in God's hands for communicating to me the unwavering love and free forgiveness of our Lord. Thank you for loving me and learning to follow Jesus with me. I love you.

CruciformPress

something new in Christian publishing

Our Books

Short. Clear. Concise. Helpful. Inspiring.
Gospel-focused. *Print, ebook, audiobook.*

Monthly Releases

A new book the first day of every month. *Licensed to Kill* is our tenth book.

Consistent Prices

Every book costs the same.

Subscription Options

Print books or ebooks delivered to you every month, at a discount.

Annual or Monthly Subscriptions

Print Book . . . . $6.49 per month
Ebook   . . . . $3.99 per month

Non-Subscription Sales

1-5 Books . . . . $8.45 each
6-50 Books . . . . $7.45 each
More than 50 Books . . . . $6.45 each

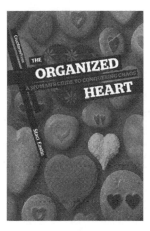

The Organized Heart
A Woman's Guide to Conquering Chaos

by Staci Eastin

**Disorganized?
You dont need more rules, the
latest technique, or a new gadget.**

**This book will show you a different,
better way. A way grounded in the
grace of God.**

"Staci Eastin packs a gracious punch, full of insights about our
disorganized hearts and lives, immediately followed by the balm of
gospel-shaped hopes. This book is ideal for accountability partners
and small groups."
**Carolyn McCulley, blogger, filmmaker, author of *Radical
Womanhood* and *Did I Kiss Marriage Goodbye?***

"Unless we understand the spiritual dimension of productivity, our
techniques will ultimately backfire. Find that dimension here. Encouraging and uplifting rather than guilt-driven, this book can help
women who want to be more organized but know that adding a new
method is not enough."
**Matt Perman, Director of Strategy at Desiring God, blogger,
author of the forthcoming book, *What's Best Next: How the
Gospel Transforms the Way You Get Things Done***

"Organizing a home can be an insurmountable challenge for a woman. The Organized Heart makes a unique connection between idols
of the heart and the ability to run a well-managed home. This is not
a how-to. Eastin looks at sin as the root problem of disorganization.
She offers a fresh new approach and one I recommend, especially to
those of us who have tried all the other self-help models and failed."
**Aileen Challies, Mom of three, and wife of blogger, author,
and pastor Tim Challies**

"But God..."
The Two Words at the Heart of the Gospel

by Casey Lute

**Just two words.
Understand their use in Scripture,
and you will never be the same.**

"Rock-solid theology packaged in an engaging and accessible form."
– *Louis Tullo, Sight Regained blog*

"Keying off of nine occurrences of "But God" in the English Bible, Casey Lute ably opens up Scripture in a manner that is instructive, edifying, encouraging, and convicting. This little book would be useful in family or personal reading, or as a gift to a friend. You will enjoy Casey's style, you will have a fresh view of some critical Scripture, and your appreciation for God's mighty grace will be deepened."
> *Dan Phillips, Pyromaniacs blog, author of* **The World-Tilting Gospel** *(forthcoming from Kregel)*

"A refreshingly concise, yet comprehensive biblical theology of grace that left this reader more in awe of the grace of God. "
> *Aaron Armstrong, BloggingTheologically.com*

""Casey Lute reminds us that nothing is impossible with God, that we must always reckon with God, and that God brings life out of death and joy out of sorrow. "
> *Thomas R. Schreiner, Professor of New Testament Interpretation, The Southern Baptist Theological Seminary*

"A mini-theology that will speak to the needs of every reader of this small but powerful book. Read it yourself and you will be blessed. Give it to a friend and you will be a blessing."
> *William Varner, Professor of Biblical Studies, The Master's College*